Child Sexual Abuse

Child Sexual Abuse

Danya Glaser and Stephen Frosh

The Dorsey Press

Chicago, IL 60604

First published 1988

Published by
MACMILLAN EDUCATION LTD
Houndmills, Basingstoke, Hampshire RG21 2XS
and London
Companies and representatives
throughout the world

Printed in Hong Kong

This U.S. edition published by
The Dorsey Press
224 South Michigan Avenue
Chicago, Illinois 60604

ISBN 0-256-07124-1 (hardcover)
ISBN 0-256-07125-X (paperback)
Library of Congress Catalog Card No. 88-70951

Contents

Contents   vii

Acknowledgements

Our primary debt is to our past and current colleagues in the Lewisham and North Southwark Child Sexual Abuse Team – Frances Campbell, Paula Collier, Julie Collison, Marion Cross, Moira Doolan, Maria Gallagher, Claire Glasscoe, Anne Harris, Pattie Rashbrook, Julian Brockless, Peter Crowley, David Edwards and Michael Wilkins. Danya Glaser would like to acknowledge the support of past colleagues in the Child Sexual Abuse team at the Hospital for Sick Children, Great Ormond Street, London, particularly Arnon Bentovim and Tilman Furniss. Finally, both authors are grateful to Suzanna Tetsell for accurately discerning and typing a sometimes indecipherable manuscript.

DANYA GLASER
STEPHEN FROSH

Introduction

Child sexual abuse has a relatively brief history in the awareness of professionals working with children. Until recently, accusations of sexual abuse originating from children were interpreted either as maliciousness or, more commonly, as the product of the child's fantasy life. Allegations of sexual abuse, and incest in particular, were often seen as instances of children's failure to distinguish between their own sexual wishes and reality. The effects of this attitude were that most cases of child sexual abuse were overlooked, even when a child tried to tell someone about what was happening, and that many adults carry with them a history of sexual victimisation which they have never been able to confide to anyone.

In the past few years, this scenario has changed dramatically. People working in all the child-care professions have become sensitised to the reality of child sexual abuse and are increasingly likely to believe children who confide in them, and to attempt to take appropriate action. General awareness of sexual abuse has also been heightened by extensive media coverage in the press and on televison and radio, all of them encouraging the victims of abuse to make themselves heard. Training courses for professionals, therapeutic techniques for helping victims and statutory child-care procedures have all been improved, even though they still warrant further development. The factors that have brought about this change in public awareness are by no means obvious. To some extent, it may have been a by-product of the increased clarity of thought and practice surrounding physical child abuse that developed during the 1970s. In addition, debates on sexuality, victimisation and power that were instituted and developed by the women's movement on both sides of the Atlantic have been crucial in challenging accepted notions of sexual practice and in drawing attention to the way women and children can be made into sexual victims. The work of the various Rape Crisis Centres in Britain has been particularly noteworthy in this regard, and it is probably fair to say that it is the arguments of feminists that have set the pace for debates in the whole area of sexual abuse.

Although child sexual abuse has become more visible as an area of professional concern, its management continues to prove complex and problematic. On the child-care side, it raises difficult questions for social workers concerning ways of protecting children, the use of fostering or other substitute care arrangements, possibilities for family rehabilitation, and liaison or co-work with the police. On the investigatory side, techniques which can be depended upon to help children give accurate and reliable information while reassuring them that they are not being blamed for the events (however they may feel about them) are still being developed. On the therapeutic side, there is a need for evaluation of the indicators for, and efficacy of, family, group and individual approaches, as well as for the further development of appropriate techniques in all these areas of treatment. Behind these uncertainties there is intense controversy over the best way to understand child sexual abuse: for example, is it properly viewed as a product of disturbed family interactions, or as a representation of the general violence of patriarchy? Finally, the personal issues raised for professionals dealing with child sexual abuse can be very powerful.

Aims and structure of the book

This book arises in large part out of debates with colleagues and clinical experience of providing both a direct service to the victims of child sexual abuse and their families, and a support and consultative service to local authority social workers engaged in such work. Our perspective is thus that of professionals involved with children and their families at the time of the abuse, rather than (as has often been the case in books on sexual abuse) the adult victims of child sexual abuse. Our aim is to provide an integrated factual and theoretical account of child sexual abuse, alongside a clear and detailed discussion of appropriate ways in which to deal with it, directed particularly at social workers but from the point of view both of statutory and therapeutic action.

This dual aim has determined the organisation of the book, *Part I* deals with the theory of child sexual abuse. Chapter 1 summarises research data on the frequency, severity and relevant characteristics of child sexual abuse. Chapters 2 and 3 outline a general model for understanding child sexual abuse and discuss the links between abuse, masculine sexuality, the status and sexuality of children, the position and actions of the mothers of abused children, and the structure of family life. *Part II* provides guidance on therapeutic and welfare practice. Chapter 4 describes the main pathways to disclosure of child sexual abuse and discusses ways of assessing suspicions and alerting signs. Chapter 5 contains a detailed look at the validation process, emphasising procedures which maximise the clarity of information obtained from a child and the effectiveness of the resulting interventions, while also being as 'therapeutic' as possible (or, at least, doing as little harm as can be done). Chapter 6 describes the post-disclosure needs of victims and their families and attempts to guide social workers through the difficult task of long-term planning. Chapter 7 presents an outline of the most promising modes of therapeutic work, with a particular emphasis on group and family work, but including discussions of individual and dyadic interventions. Finally, Chapter 8 considers professionals' needs, interprofessional roles and relationships, and the place of specialist child sexual abuse teams. One important area that is not specifically addressed here, because it falls outside the reactive brief of social workers, is that of prevention of child sexual abuse. It is our belief that while there is considerable virtue in enterprises which aim to give children guidance in ways of protecting themselves against sexual abuse, genuine primary prevention awaits some central changes in our social attitudes to children and, most significantly, to the sexual socialisation of men.

The styles of Parts I and II are rather different, as a result of their different contents. Part I is more discursive and argumentative; Part II is more 'instructive', and attempts to provide clear principles and guidelines upon which a professional response can be built. The suggestions in Part II are informed by the arguments of Part I, as well as by research and our own experience.

Note on pronominal usage

Since the vast majority of child sexual abusers are men, we have throughout the book referred to abusers as 'he'. Since most victims are girls, in Part II we have referred to victims as 'she'. However, in the theoretical sections of Part I we are concerned to present as full a picture as possible of the parameters of child sexual abuse. As this includes the information that a substantial number of victims are boys (possibly around a third of the total), we have adopted the usage 'she or he' for this section of the book.

Part I

Understanding Child Sexual Abuse

1

Myth and Reality: the Dimensions of Child Sexual Abuse

In recent years there has been a welcome improvement in awareness and understanding of child sexual abuse and its associated phenomena. A number of carefully conducted surveys have clarified the incidence of child sexual abuse, revealing that it is not, as previously assumed, a rare occurrence, nor one that is confined to obviously 'disturbed' segments of the population. It has also become clear that many instances of sexual abuse occur within families and that most abusers are known to their child victims, often being relatives or adult friends. The 'warning signs' of sexual abuse are becoming more familiar, and professionals are now somewhat less likely to dismiss as fantasy stories told to them by children. The aims and principles of statutory and therapeutic work with the victims of sexual abuse and their families have become matters for serious and vigorous debate.

Despite these real advances, there remains a large number of uncertainties and confusions surrounding child sexual abuse. To some extent, this may be due to the particular aura of 'incest' and the problems adults commonly have in dealing with sexuality, both in themselves and in children. In addition, child sexual abuse is a difficult area to research, since secrecy, shame and guilt are among its principal components. Furthermore, child sexual abuse provokes strong emotions, because it raises significant issues about how children are treated, about sexuality and about power – issues that are central to many debates, such as those surrounding feminist critiques of contemporary society. For these reasons it is important

3

to establish what is known about the actual dimensions of child sexual abuse – its frequency, the characteristics of victims and abusers, its experienced severity and its long-term impact. This is the purpose of this chapter.

Definitions

There appears to be no universally accepted definition of what constitutes child sexual abuse, although there is a large number of helpful *ad hoc* formulations and operational guidelines. These derive mainly from research studies in which investigators have attempted to formulate specific, operational definitions which are nevertheless broad enough to include a wide range of abusive and potentially abusive experiences. The clarity of some of these definitions is obviously helpful, but the variations between those adopted in different studies are sometimes quite considerable. Variations of this kind are particularly significant because they may explain some of the variations in reported statistics of child sexual abuse. In addition, the rather broad nature of many research-based definitions may not provide the best guidelines for questions pertinent to planning for mental health practice: questions such as when is intervention necessary.

The best definitions currently used combine a clear specification of what is meant by 'sexual' with some guidance on the age of developmental level of the participants, sometimes with a clause concerning the experienced aversiveness of the activity and the elements which make it abusive. Thus, Finkelhor (1984) defines 'sexual victimisation' as 'sexual encounters of children under age thirteen with persons at least five years older than themselves and encounters of children thirteen to sixteen with persons at least ten years older'. Sexual encounters could be 'intercourse, anal-genital contact, fondling, or an encounter with an exhibitionist' (pp. 23–4). Others have broadened the definition of 'sexual' to include any activity that brings gratification to the partner. Baker and Duncan (1985), for example, presented the following definition to the (adult) respondents in their survey:

> A child (anyone under sixteen years) is sexually abused when another person, who is sexually mature, involves the child in any activity which

the other person expects to lead to their sexual arousal. (p. 458)

A few definitions incorporate a notion of developmental or social norms and of the child's ability to consent to sexual contact, the most influential being that of Schechter and Roberge (1976):

> sexual abuse is defined as the involvement of dependent, developmentally immature children and adolescents in sexual activities they do not truly comprehend, to which they are unable to give informed consent, or that violate the social taboos of family roles. (p. 60)

Finally, the 'child sexual abuse working definition' provided by SCOSAC (1984) usefully ties together most of the various strands present in all the other definitions, and deserves to be quoted in full:

> Any child below the age of consent may be deemed to have been sexually abused when a sexually mature person has, by design or by neglect of their usual societal or specific responsibilities in relation to the child, engaged or permitted the engagement of that child in any activity of a sexual nature which is intended to lead to the sexual gratification of the sexually mature person. This definition pertains whether or not this activity involves explicit coercion by any means, whether or not it involves genital or physical contact, whether or not initiated by the child, and whether or not there is discernible harmful outcome in the short term.

A number of points arise from these various definitions, but three stand out as central. The first concerns what is to be called 'sexual': is, for example, an exhibitionist or voyeuristic episode not specifically construed by a child as sexual to be included in the rubric? Or should it simply be labelled 'abuse', or perhaps 'attempted abuse'? The difficulty surrounds not just these particular acts, but all attempts to list specific activities rather than provide a general criterion, for it is not clear that every child will identify the same acts as sexual, nor that all children will relate to them as exploitative or harmful. For this reason, the intention of the abuser is probably a useful main criterion for what is to be called sexual abuse, as in SCOSAC's reference to the 'sexual gratification' of the adult. This implies that children can be abused without being aware of it (for instance, in some forms of voyeurism), but it usefully draws attention to a central element in sexual abuse: that it is something carried out by the adult for his own sexual purposes, taking the child as an object in the action. This also highlights the way different forms of abuse that vary markedly in degree of severity and impact might nevertheless have common underlying purposes and psychodynamic structures.

A second issue concerns that of the age and developmental level of the child and the abuser. Most definitions select a chronological age to define the limits of abuse, usually legally rather than psychologically designated, for instance sixteen or eighteen or 'the age of consent'. Several definitions also postulate an age difference of about five years or more for sexual contact to be regarded as abusive. Clearly, these are imprecise guidelines; they require greater specificity for research purposes and are complicated to apply in individual cases. For example, a girl may well not be able to defend herself when faced with the threats of a teenage boy who is less than five years older than herself. The point here is that all cases of sexual abuse involve the use of coercion in an explicit or implicit way, and this is indeed a central factor in designating it as abusive. For this reason, Schechter and Roberge's (1976) phrase 'not able to give informed consent' seems a more valuable marker of abuse than any precise age; it demands an evaluation of developmental competence and the power relationship involved when making the judgement of abuse. Thus, a young child who does not resist an advance by an adult would still be regarded as having been abused because of the child's lack of knowledge of the social meanings and psychological effects of sexual encounters; also, her or his trust in and dependency upon adults mean that she or he would not be in a position to give informed consent. Conversely, a teenager who might have at least some of the requisite social knowledge would still be abused if her or his position with respect to the other was one of dependency, or being coerced, so that a free choice – informed *consent* – was not an available option. All the attempts made to include a measure of the degree of 'unwantedness' of the sexual contact are incorporated in this argument about informed consent.

The third issue arises out of this last point and is significant for considerations of the nature of child sexual abuse and its relationships to other forms of abuse, for example rape of adult women. This is the issue of the power relationship that pertains between the abuser and his victim. All forms of abuse have at their centre the exploitation of a power differential; this may be explicit and obvious, as where direct physical force is used, or it may be more subtle, playing on the dependency of the victim – the most common scenario in child sexual abuse. The SCOSAC definition to some extent recognises this in its reference to the adult's 'usual societal or specific responsibilities to the child', but it does not make any link with the more general 'politics' of abuse. Power is inherent in all relations between people, expressed in different forms and varying across different domains (one person may have more power in one area, a second in another). It is linked to dependence, although usually distinguishable from it: one does not need to be dependent on another to be physically coerced by him. The existence of abuse is therefore partially defined by the use of a position of power to manipulate another for one's own gratification and against the dictates of the well-being of the other. This is true in all situations, linking child sexual abuse with other examples of power manipulation.

The question that arises here is whether there is something distinct about child sexual abuse that differentiates it from other instances in which power is exploited for sexual ends. The argument in favour of such a differentiation is that in the case of sexual contact between a child and an adult there is no need to explore the specific relationship that surrounds the two protagonists. This is because children are *structurally* dependent on adults; that is, their dependence is one of the factors that defines them as children. Sexual activity between an adult and a child thus always designates an exploitation of power; in this respect, it differs from other forms of sexual encounter and can never be anything but abuse. Thus, there is no need to name the power relationship in definitions of child sexual abuse, as it is already implicit in the status of the child *qua* child. This is an important argument, as it draws attention to some of the prime ethical justifications for intervening to prevent adult–child sexual contacts: dependency is a defining, necessary element of childhood, and children have a right to enter into it with trust. Contravention of this special right is always abuse. There is no other relationship in which the power-dependency structure is so clear and so universal, and in which trust is so integral to dependency; in addition, the degree of difference in physical and emotional maturity between (especially pre-pubertal) children and their abusers is unique to child sexual abuse. For these reasons, the sexual abuse of children is at least quantitatively different from other abusive situations, even though all abuse involves an exploitation of power, often legitimised by forces embedded in the social structure. For example, many employer–employee encounters have the same power-dependency structure; more generally, the position of women in our society is still one that usually makes them dependent upon men (particularly within marriage) and hence available to coercion.

The clinical utility of definitions

While it may be clear in principle that an adult engaging in sexual activities with a child should be designated as abusing that child, in practice it is sometimes difficult to decide whether the contact is actually abusive or not. For example, the boundaries between appropriate affectionate and inappropriate sexual physical contact between adults and children may be difficult to draw; it may not be clear whether an adult is deriving sexual gratification from an action with a child; it may be even less clear whether a child is aware that anything untoward has taken place at all. In these marginal or unclear instances, the question of whether intervention is appropriate or not, and if so what type or degree of intervention, may be very difficult to answer. All this is in addition to the more widespread problem of obtaining clear information concerning the precise nature of the contact between a child and an adult, a problem to be addressed in detail in Chapters 4 and 5.

A number of points arise from these considerations. First, there are many instances in which the adult–child encounter falls within the definitions given earlier. In these situations, such definitions provide useful heuristics for naming the encounter as abuse, and also clarify issues such as whether the severity of the incident or the child's active participation in it should influence the name given to it. The view adopted here is that the degree of coercion, genital contact, child activity or immediate outcome are all irrelevant to the naming of an adult–child sexual encounter as abusive. These encounters are legitimately called 'sexual abuse' because children cannot give informed consent to them; they always represent an exploitation of power and a betrayal of trust. Secondly, there is a real difficulty with some borderline cases where it is unclear whether something is to be labelled 'affectionate physical contact' or 'sexual interference'. Sometimes these can be differentiated by reference to the child's feelings. If a child is made to feel uncomfortable or worried by the physical attentions she or he is receiving, then this signals something amiss. Whether it is always sexual abuse that is going on in this situation is a moot point, perhaps only to be decided by unravelling the motives of the adult, but at the very least it is inappropriate contact. Otherwise, the general rule that equates 'sexual contact' with some form of genital involvement is a useful one where questions of the appropriateness of physical encounters are raised.

Thirdly, there is the question of when intervention is necessary. This will be described in more practical terms in Part II of this book, but the general answer here can only be 'always'. The rationale for this derives from the currently available data on the effects of child sexual abuse. This is reviewed at the end of this chapter but its general message can be summarised here: child sexual abuse is usually experienced aversively by the victim; it often has serious consequences for the child; these consequences may be long term; they can be ameliorated by sensitive responses on the part of family members or professionals. Perhaps most importantly for questions of intervention, it is very difficult to predict whether an experience of abuse will have long-term damaging consequences for a particular child; therefore, therapeutic assessments as well as protective interventions are jutified in all cases. Defining something as clearly sexual abuse does not necessarily alter its effects on a child (although it might, because of the impact of social responses), but it does alert professionals to the possible severity of the situation, and the care with which it must be treated.

A final point of interest here is the relationship between child sexual abuse and other forms of child abuse. There are some systematic links: for example, sexual abuse sometimes involves physical coercion and injury; adults who were sexually abused as children have a heightened probability of neglecting or physically abusing their children (Goodwin, 1982). But there are also differences: many cases of sexual abuse do not involve physical hurt, and some have an affectionate context which is unusual in non-accidental injury cases. In general, and except in instances of associated physical injury or rape by strangers, child sexual abuse is best classed alongside severe emotional abuse in terms of its structure and effects.

The frequency of child sexual abuse

There are two kinds of information that currently provide guidance on the frequency with which child sexual abuse occurs. The first of these is data derived from studies of children referred to police, social services, doctors or therapeutic agencies and who are discovered to have been sexually abused. These studies suggest quite a low rate of child sexual abuse. For example, a British survey by Mrazek, Lynch and Bentovim (1983) of 1599 family doctors, police surgeons, paediatricians and child psychiatrists uncovered a total of 1072 child sexual abuse cases seen by these professionals in the year 1977–8. This, if a valid finding, would give an incidence figure (number of new cases in the population) of 1500 per year, which represents one child in every six thousand. Over the entire childhood period (up to fifteen years old), the authors estimate that three children in every thousand are recognised as sexually abused. However, there are some difficulties with the Mrazek *et al.* study: for example, the overall response rate from the professionals circulated was only 39 per cent, with a mere 16 per cent of family doctors returning their forms. There is also a more general problem which plagues all studies of this kind and which severely limits the generalisability of their findings. This is simply that they are restricted to cases that have been identified and passed through the formal professional channels. As such, they grossly underestimate the true frequency of sexual abuse: at every stage, from disclosure by a child to response by a professional to registration as a statistic, there are reasons why sexual abuse is neglected and overlooked. To give just two examples: many abused children are too frightened, ashamed or confused ever to tell anyone of their plight; similarly, in the present as in the past, many professionals are too frightened, ashamed, confused or simply unskilled to respond appropriately when a child does begin to talk. Studies such as that of Mrazek *et al* are useful as indicators of the number of cases that come to professional attention; they say little about the true rates of abuse in the general population. In any event, it appears that increased awareness of, and publicity concerning, child sexual abuse may be as important determinants of referral rates as are the actual numbers of children involved. For instance, a review of referrals of child sexual abuse cases to paediatricians in Leeds over a six-year period was reported by Wild (1986). These referrals increased from none in 1979 to 50 in 1984 and 161 in 1985. In 1984, abuse was confirmed or considered to be probable in 30 of the 50 referrals (28 girls); in 1985 the equivalent figure was 106. Similarly, the NSPCC in Britain experienced a 90 per cent increase in reported cases of child sexual abuse between 1984 and 1985, and a comparable futher increase in 1986, presumably a product of the increased publicity that surrounded sexual abuse during that period.

The second source of data on the frequency of child sexual abuse is a series of population studies in which adults are surveyed on their sexual experiences as children. There are a few very good studies of this kind, which vary in their findings but which all indicate that child sexual abuse is a common and destructive phenomenon. The best available British investigation, reported by Baker and Duncan (1985), involved a detailed interview of 2019 women and men aged fifteen and over, selected to be a nationally representative sample. Each person was presented with a definition of sexual abuse which was based on the notion of someone sexually mature involving a child in 'any activity which the other person expects to lead to their sexual arousal. This might involve intercourse, touching, exposure of the sexual organs, showing pornographic material or talking about sexual things in an erotic way' (p. 459) – a notably broad range of activities. Interviewees were asked if they had had such experiences before the age of sixteen; 10 per cent of them (206 individuals) said they had, 77 per cent said they had not, and 13 per cent refused to answer. Baker and Duncan note that these results suggest that there are currently more than four and a half million adults in Great Britain who, according to their criteria, were sexually abused as children, while a potential 1 117 000 children will be so abused by the age of fifteen. Other British data suggest even larger numbers. West (1985) found that 46 per cent of the 600 women that he surveyed reported being sexually abused as children; in Hall's (1985) sample of 1236 women, 21 per cent remembered being sexually abused as children, with one-third of these saying that it had occurred more than once.

If the British studies seem to suggest an extremely high rate of child sexual abuse, the best similar studies from the United States imply that they might in fact be underestimating the true rate. Russell (1983) conducted an interview study of a random sample of 930 women aged eighteen and over in San Francisco in 1978, using a definition of sexual abuse that included only experiences involving sexual contact (from petting to rape). Thirty-eight per cent of the sample, a total of 357 women, reported experiencing at least one incident of sexual abuse before age eighteen, with 29 per cent (258 women) before age fourteen. Breaking down these figures into 'extrafamilial' and 'intrafamilial' abuse, 16 per cent of women reported at least one experience of intrafamilial abuse by age eighteen (12 per cent by fourteen), while 31 per cent reported at least one experience of extrafamilial abuse by eighteen (20 per cent by fourteen). If the definition of sexual abuse is extended to include non-contact experiences such as exhibitionism (as in many other studies), an astronomical 54 per cent of the sample had been abused by age eighteen. While some American studies have reported lower rates than those found by Russell (e.g. Finkelhor, 1979), it is clear that sexual abuse is so common as to be, for many girls, a 'normal' part of growing up.

There are clear problems with the population surveys described above. Their definitions of sexual abuse vary and are sometimes very broad, possibly leading to inflated statistics. Reliance on questionnaires and interviews with often uncertain psychometric characteristics calls into question the validity of the findings. Most importantly, asking adults to recall experiences from their childhood, especially emotionally sensitive experiences, produces notoriously unreliable findings, a situation compounded by the impossibility of checking their accuracy by reference to any independent source. Nevertheless, the results of several separate surveys with carefully selected populations, using trained interviewers and reasonably well-constructed questionnaires, all show a very high frequency of child sexual abuse, far higher than would be assumed from the numbers seeking help. Sexual abuse is no fiction, nor a bandwagon which will roll away when the next interesting problem appears on the scene: it is a real phenomenon, and its magnitude is only beginning to be recognised.

Victims and abusers

All surveys have shown a preponderance of girls over boys among victims of sexual abuse, with the actual proportions varying within a fairly narrow range. In the study of college students by Finkelhor (1979), the rates of sexual abuse experienced in childhood were twice as high for women (19 per cent) as for men (9 per cent). Baker and Duncan's (1985) British survey obtained abuse rates of 12 per cent for girls and 8 per cent for boys, roughly in line with other findings. Clinical studies tend to show much lower proportions of boys than these, perhaps due to varying definitions as well as possible inhibiting factors specific to reporting of sexual abuse of boys (e.g. that older boys may be socialised out of reporting even more strongly than are girls). In general, the most reasonable conclusion from the available data is that boys are quite frequently sexually abused, at a rate between a fifth and a half that for girls.

All studies which have investigated the question of the gender of abusers have uncovered only a very small proportion of female abusers, at most 4 per cent where the victims are girls (Russell, 1983) and 20 per cent where the victims are boys (Finkelhor, 1984). Finkelhor (1984) notes:

> Especially since contacts with female children occur with at least twice or three times the frequency as male children, the presumption that sexual abusers are primarily men seems clearly supported. (p. 177)

In coming to these conclusions, Finkelhor suggests that the male preponderence is unlikely to be due simply to abuses by women going undetected, because they apply to retrospective non-clinical surveys, and also because they remain even when only sexual 'contacts' rather than 'abuses' are asked about. In all studies, it is men who appear as the adults in sexual contact with children. Child sexual abuse is, in this sense, a phenomenon connected with the sexuality of men.

There are a number of other descriptors of victims and abusers which are of some importance both for theory and practice, but which do not require extended discussion here. There are few data on class and ethnic distribution; those which exist suggest that child sexual abuse is more common overall in poorer families, but show a more middle-class distribution than other forms of child abuse. It seems likely that child sexual abuse is about equally common in different ethnic groups, although the data here is conflicting and limited to American samples (e.g. Wyatt, 1985). The most common time for the sexual abuse of children to begin is when the victims are aged between eight and fourteen years, although the range extends right down to infancy. There are some variations in the age data reported in different studies, but the clear conclusion that arises from them all (e.g. Baker and Duncan, 1985; Wild, 1986) is that child sexual abuse is not something that occurs primarily to post-pubescent adolescents.

As is now becoming well recognised, advice to children that

warns them only to keep clear of strangers and unfamiliar places will not protect them very effectively against sexual abuse. In Baker and Duncan's (1985) study, 49 per cent of abusers were known to their victims, and 14 per cent of all reported abuse took place within the family. Girls were more likely to have been abused by parents, grandparents or siblings, while boys were more at risk from people outside the family but known to them. Russell (1983) found that abusers were mostly not relatives, but also were not likely to be strangers: only 11 per cent were total strangers, 29 per cent were relatives, and 60 per cent were known to the victims but unrelated to them. Forty-two women in this study reported being sexually abused by their fathers before age eighteen, which translates as 4.5 per cent of Russell's random sample. Within the extrafamilial abuse group, 40 per cent of abusers were classified as 'authority figures'.

As well as not being safe with supposedly safe people, children are not safe in supposedly safe places. Twenty-six per cent of the abused children in the study by DeJong *et al.* (1983) were assaulted in their own home, a further 21 per cent in the home of the abuser – who was generally known to the child. Many abusers are quite young themselves: for example, Walmsly and White (1979) found that over half of their sample of 709 males convicted for unlawful sexual intercourse with girls aged thirteen to fifteen were themselves under twenty-one (British data); it is not clear how similar the age-range of abusers of young children may be. Finally, it appears from Wild's (1986) Leeds study that some children are members of sex rings operating for money. In seven of the thirty confirmed or probable cases referred to paediatricians in 1984, the girls had taken part in child sex rings, usually as ringleaders.

> With the help of two or three deputies they had provided sexual favours for, and introduced younger girls to, the male abuser, usually for money. Several of the ringleaders were known to have been sexually abused within the family home. Each sex ring contained an average of twenty girls, making this an important type of abuse that appears to be widespread. (p. 1115)

A number of family factors are associated with increased likelihood of child sexual abuse. The issue of family involvement will be discussed in detail in Chapter 3; only a few statistically relevant predictors will be mentioned here. In his analysis of his female student sample data, Finkelhor (1984) found the strongest correlate of sexual victimisation to be having a stepfather: this was the situation for 47 per cent of abused girls. To a considerable extent, this represents risk from the stepfather himself: stepfathers were five times more likely to sexually abuse their daughters than were natural fathers. Russell (1983) similarly found that one in six women with a stepfather had been abused by him in childhood, compared to a rate of one in forty for biological fathers. But Finkelhor points to other associated risks which make girls with stepfathers more vulnerable; for instance, they were five times as likely to be abused by friends of one or other parent. There were also certain attributes of mothers that made their daughters more likely to be abused. Women who reported that their mothers were 'emotionally distant, often ill, or unaffectionate' were at higher risk, as were those who grew up without their natural mothers (though not those whose mothers worked). Victimised girls were much more likely to have had mothers who were sexually punitive; a father's conservative values and paucity of physical affection also increased the risk.

Finkelhor's study also reveals no difference in the amount of family violence observed or experienced by abused and non-abused girls. There may be some differences between these factors and those relevant for abused boys, who are perhaps more likely to live with their fathers or with any father-figure in the home (Pierce and Pierce, 1985), but in general Finkelhor's findings make the unsurprising point that sexual abuse is more likely to occur to girls growing up in families in which there is chronic stress, lack of physical openness, poor protection from the mother, and contact with sexually promiscuous men. There is also clinical evidence that siblings of sexually abused children may be at increased risk themselves, and that child sexual abuse may coexist with other forms of child abuse (see Nelson, 1987).

The severity of child sexual abuse

There is considerable evidence that child sexual abuse is an aversive experience for children, often having harmful effects in the long term. First, although for many children sexual abuse occurs on only one occasion (63 per cent of Baker and Duncan's (1985) group and 75 per cent of that of Wyatt, 1985), a large number experience prolonged or multiple abuse of a serious kind. In the Baker and

Duncan sample, 23 per cent of abused respondents reported repeated abuse by the same person, while 14 per cent reported multiple abuse by a number of people.

Secondly, although only a minority of abuses involve full sexual intercourse (5 per cent in the Baker and Duncan survey and 4 per cent in that of Finkelhor, 1979), most include some form of physical contact and in some instances force is used. Russell (1983) made a careful distinction between different degrees of severity of abuses inflicted on her sample of women. 'Very serious sexual abuse' included experiences ranging from forced penile–vaginal penetration to attempted fellatio, cunnilingus and anal intercourse; 'serious sexual abuse' included experiences ranging from forced digital penetration of the vagina to non-forceful attempted breast contact or simulated intercourse (p. 140). Twenty-three per cent of all incidents of intrafamilial child sexual abuse were classified as 'very serious' and 41 per cent as 'serious'; the respective figures for extrafamilial abuse were 53 per cent and 27 per cent. For sexual abuse by stepfathers, the proportion of 'very serious' abuses was 47 per cent.

Thirdly, most children experience sexual contact with adults as aversive. In Baker and Duncan's (1985) abused group, 54 per cent said that the abuse had had a harmful effect on their lives; those abused within the family felt more harmed, with 67 per cent reporting the experience as damaging, while the equivalent figure for those abused by fathers was 75 per cent. Perceived damage was worse for women than for men; it was also worse when the abuse began before the child was ten years old, and when it was repeated. Only 4 per cent of the sample said the abuse had improved the quality of their lives; this represents seven people, five of whom were male, three of whom had been abused by women, and none of whom had been abused within the family. It is important to note that all these studies are retrospective: it may be that more of the experiences had pleasurable components than the adult respondents recalled or were willing to admit. This does not, however, make them any easier to tolerate: rather, clinical experience with children suggests that sexual encounters which are experienced as partially pleasurable may be harder to deal with, as they increase the likelihood of the child feeling guilty and confused.

Finally, there is much evidence that the long-term effects of child sexual abuse can be harmful. Sexually abused children commonly show negative emotional reactions such as depression, guilt or lowered self-esteem; sexual abuse is also linked to phobias and nightmares, restlessness, bedwetting, school refusal, adolescent pregnancies, suicide attempts – the whole gamut of childhood psychological difficulties (Tsai *et al.*, 1979; Goodwin, 1982). Victims of sexual abuse may sexualise all their relationships in an attempt to gain affection; in adolescence this can lead to a self-destructive pattern of promiscuity with a succession of abusive relationships. In the long term, case studies and questionnaire surveys indicate that adults (particularly women, on whom most of the information has been collected) who have been sexually abused as children have impaired self-esteem, including sexual self-esteem (Finkelhor, 1984), are more likely to become drug or alcohol addicts (Benward and Densen-Gerber, 1975), and are commonly found among psychotherapy patients, often appearing disturbed to a 'psychotic' or at least borderline extent (e.g. Herman and Hirschman, 1977). Other studies have revealed high rates of childhood sexual abuse in the histories of adult rape victims and of women abused by their husbands (e.g. Russell, 1982). Most significantly, perhaps, for social workers and other professionals working with children, it seems that victims of child sexual abuse are more likely than others to have children who are themselves abused, both physically (Goodwin, 1982) and sexually (CIBA, 1984). To some extent the latter is a direct link, whereby people who have been sexually abused themselves go on to abuse their children: this happens primarily with male victims, who often seem to replicate the desolate patterns of parenting to which they have been exposed, which include an image of children as sexually exploitable. There is also a powerful indirect link, whereby girls who are sexually abused grow up to have daughters who are sexually abused by other people. This is discussed further in Chapter 3, but in outline the suggestion is that the experience of abuse increases women's vulnerability to sexually exploitative men and reduces their ability to protect their children. In various ways, therefore, child sexual abuse can harm several generations.

Evidence such as that outlined above provides a rationale for intervention in child sexual abuse. It is not, however, the situation that *all* sexually abused children have bad outcomes, although it is clear that many do, with approximately two-thirds of abused children showing moderate or severe evidence of behavioural and psychological disturbance (Conte and Berliner, 1987). There is probably much to be learnt from comparisons of 'good-outcome' and 'poor-outcome' groups. The best available study in this area is that of Tsai *et al.* (1979), who compared a group of women seeking therapy for problems associated with childhood molestation (the 'clinical' group) with a second group of women molested as children, but who had never sought therapy and considered themselves well adjusted. There were no differences between the groups along some dimensions that might have been thought relevant, for instance the proportions abused by close relatives, the age of first molestation, or the length of time that elapsed prior to disclosure. The groups did differ, however, in the following ways:

(a) women in the clinical group had been on average significantly older than their counterparts in the non-clinical group at the termination of abuse (12.4 years versus 9.2). This also meant that they had suffered abuse of longer duration (4.7 versus 2.5 years);

(b) clinical group members tended to have been abused with greater frequency (50 per cent were abused two or more times per week);

(c) the clinical group reported stronger negative feelings associated with the abuse – 'more pressure to participate, more guilt, greater pain, greater dislike for the molestor, and stronger feelings of being "upset" at the time of the molestation'. (p. 415)

Tsai *et al.* also asked the members of the non-clinical group what they thought had helped them most. Two factors stood out in their answers. First, support from friends and family 'in the form of assurance that the woman had not been at fault, had no reason to feel guilty, and was still a worthwhile person'; second, sympathetic and understanding sexual partners who helped the woman distinguish between her abuser and other men (p. 416).

In general, this study again suggests the value of intervention: if sexual abuse is occurring, the priority is to stop it, as duration appears to be a significant determinant of severity of outcome. In addition, anything that makes the child feel less guilty, more accepted and supported by others close to her, may have long-term beneficial effects. These, then, are important considerations for social workers and other professionals working with sexually abused children.

2

A Multi-faceted Phenomenon: Sexuality and Child Sexual Abuse

Theorising sexual abuse

A comprehensive theory of child sexual abuse will be a complex matter, including elements related to broad social processes as well as to intimate personal relations. To some extent, child sexual abuse is a social phenomenon, linked to general attitudes and practices towards children and also to the ways sexual relationships are organised and regulated in any particular society. While it is important to take this into account in any full model of how abuse occurs, for clinical and social work purposes it is probably more useful to consider 'micro-social' features, particularly the psychology of individual protagonists (especially the abuser) and the interpersonal networks in which they are embedded. In this and the following chapter we explore the forces that produce child sexual abuse at this micro-social level, focusing on the sexuality of men and of children, and on the family processes that make abuse more likely to occur. Explanatory models of this kind are extremely contentious and raise numerous general and political issues in their wake, a situation which often gives rise to polarised views, particularly between adherents of feminist and family systems viewpoints (see Dale *et al.*, 1986). We therefore wish to spell out our model in advance, before the detailed discussion.

The argument we offer is that it is important to distinguish between the *immediate cause* of sexual abuse, which lies in the psychology of the abuser, and the constellation of relationships,

19

social arrangements and values that make children more or less likely to be victimised. There are significant theoretical, practical, psychological and ethical differences between abusing a child and failing to protect a child against abuse. In essence, we follow the suggestions of Finkelhor (1984), who describes a 'four preconditions' model of sexual abuse which distinguishes between the 'motivation to sexually abuse' and various inhibiting factors which have to be overcome before abuse actually occurs. The factors included under the heading of 'motivation' are all related to masculine sexuality, either internal to an individual (e.g. how much arousal a man feels towards children) or at the level of socio-cultural values. The 'inhibiting factors' are divided into three classes: internal (e.g. moral values), external (e.g. supervision of the child by others) and the child's own resistance. Finkelhor lists numerous factors that can lead to the overcoming of these inhibitions: for example, internal inhibitions may be overcome by alcohol; the absence or illness of the child's mother may remove a significant external inhibition; coercion may force a child to cease to resist. It is possible to take issue with various of Finkelhor's specific suggestions, but his overall model is a very helpful one. It locates the general source of child sexual abuse in masculine sexuality, and it makes clear that it is the abuser who is responsible for a specific act of abuse when it occurs. It also takes account of the evidence that exists for contributory influences to abuse stemming from the emotional needs of others in a family, but it again places these in an appropriate perspective, as factors which are exploited or which make a child more vulnerable, rather than as abusive acts in themselves.

In the next section, we give a more detailed account of those elements in masculine sexuality that are relevant for understanding child sexual abuse. In this, a distinction must be maintained between general factors which make abuse a possibility for all men, and influences on individuals which might make a specific man abuse a particular child.

The sexuality of men

The most common image of men who sexually abuse children is that of the 'dirty old man', the stranger who deceives youngsters and interferes with them as an expression of his own degeneracy. The statistics presented in Chapter 1 make it apparent that this stereotype cannot be an accurate one: most victims are abused by someone they know, frequently from within the family. In addition, abusers are often quite young, in many cases below twenty. It is not even clear that all abusers are sexually frustrated in the sense of having no alternative outlets for their desires: at least some of those who have sexual relations with children are very promiscuous. Variations such as these should promote caution in drawing up any simple classification system for describing abusive men; nevertheless, there have been some attempts to categorise men who abuse children according to behavioural or personality attributes. A popular example is Weinberg's (1955) scheme, which distinguishes between (a) 'endogamic' abusers, who are oriented inwards, towards their families over whom they keep a tightly possessive hold; (b) 'psychopathic' abusers, who treat all people within their power as sexual possessions; and (c) 'paedophilic' abusers, whose psychological immaturity makes them fixate upon children as their sexual objects. Although this schema holds some interest, its drawback is that it suggests that children are abused only by particular groups of abnormal men, who may themselves have had pathogenic backgrounds, and who are distinct from other men. In fact, abusive men form an extremely heterogeneous group. For instance, some seem to be motivated primarily by sexual desires, while others are motivated by needs for closeness or by aggression (Finkelhor, 1979), or by sentimental images of children (Weeks, 1985). Some may be fearful of sexual contact with adults (Howells, 1979); some may be violent, while others are unassertive (Langevin, 1985); some are paedophilic in the sense of having an explicit preference for children as sexual partners, while others have only an attraction towards the specific child with whom they become involved, or have simply taken advantage of a particular situation (Abel *et al.*, 1979; Langevin, 1985). Many abusive acts against children are committed when men have been drinking, and there is some suggestion that more men in this group may be alcoholic (e.g. Christie *et al.*, 1978), although there is also general agreement among researchers and clinicians that the role of alcohol is a disinhibiting rather than a causal one. Some men prefer young children as their targets, others adolescents; some are homosexual, more are heterosexual; some abuse any child who may be available.

There seem to be no particular systematic differences between these groups of men, nor even between those who are incestuous and those who take children outside their family as their targets (Finkelhor, 1984).

These variations in the attributes of men who sexually abuse children present a picture of them as generally 'normal', showing a range of sexual perceptions and responses that are characteristic of non-abusive men. This does not mean that no attempt should be made to explain how these particular men come to abuse children, and in fact some useful suggestions have been made in this area. For instance, Finkelhor (1984) presents a scheme of abuser-psychology based around four underlying factors: emotional congruence (which refers to the way sexual contact with a child can be emotionally gratifying for an adult, perhaps because of the sense of power that it brings), sexual arousal to children (possibly produced by the effects of victimisation and legitimised by pornography), blockage of alternative avenues for gratification, and disinhibition of common social constraints. This scheme is an instance of an attempt to describe the make-up of men who sexually abuse children which does not rely on simple personality categorisations nor on a series of pathological traits. Rather, Finkelhor argues for the importance of a variety of specific experiences (e.g. being abused oneself in childhood) interacting with internal attributes (e.g. lack of relationship skills) and wider factors that contribute more generally to the sexual orientation and socialisation of men (e.g. pornography, denigration of women and children as property). Thus, Finkelhor's approach acknowledges that any particular child abuser will have idiosyncratic aspects to his character and experience that are relevant to the abuse; but it suggests that there are also normative factors in the socialisation of men that help explain why such abuse is widespread.

A particular issue of some importance concerns the extent to which violence is an attribute of sexually abusive men. One of the common stereotypes of 'child molesters' and incestuous fathers is that they are weak, passive men who inveigle children into sex with them through indirect means that often play on their own dependency. However, there is evidence that violence is commonly used by at least some paedophiles, and that other sexually abusing men (e.g. incestuous fathers) may also show violent aspects to their behaviour. This is certainly true of imprisoned offenders (e.g.

Christie *et al.*, 1978; Langevin, 1985), although these men may be a special group, with their violent behaviour possibly being a reason why they have been caught, prosecuted and incarcerated. Non-violent abusers may be less well represented in the prison population, but quite common outside.

One consistent strand in the literature on sexual abuse is a picture of incestuous fathers as dominating and authoritarian at home, while often presenting a meek and compliant face to external authorities. Herman (1981), for instance, presents data from a series of interviews with adult victims of incest which underlines the authoritarianism of the fathers involved. They appear as relatively competent at work and in their social lives, but exerting stringent control over their wives and daughters, if necessary dominating their families by the use of force. Herman also points to the addictive nature of the incestuous contact and the way that the unhappiness of the girl sometimes seems to contribute to the father's enjoyment – suggesting that the exploitation of power might in itself be a motivation for sexual abuse in some cases. Jackson (1982) makes a point which links this with wider issues of masculine sexuality:

> Child molesters and child rapists are almost invariably men who have learnt to express their sexuality through aggression, to seek power over others and to be attracted to the vulnerable. (p. 173)

The point is that this may be true of all men: 'violence is not just learnt as male activity. It is part of what actually shapes the contours of masculinity' (Eardley, 1985, p. 97). It is also part of the normal experience of childhood in our culture: over 84 per cent of American parents use physical punishment as a means of disciplining their children (Straus *et al.*, 1981); in Britain, corporal punishment is regarded by many as acceptable within the home and legitimate at school.

Women as well as men have power over children, but women rarely sexually abuse them. What is it exactly about the sexuality of men that makes children so vulnerable? Probably the most common image of masculine sexuality is what Hollway (1984) calls the 'male sexual drive discourse', the notion that 'men's sexuality is directly produced by a biological drive, the function of which is to ensure the reproduction of the species' (p. 231). This is a view of masculine sexuality that is often adopted by abusers themselves as a way of freeing them from responsibility for their desires and actions. Ward (1984) gives the 'male sexual drive discourse' its more accurate, if simplified, name:

> The ideology of rape says that male sexuality is innately active, aggressive and insatiable; that female sexuality is innately passive, receptive and inhibited. (p. 81)

Viewing masculine sexuality as something pre-determined is a way of avoiding examination of the processes through which it becomes constructed. In particular, it leads to neglect of the characteristics of sexuality that make it both central and problematic for many men. At the core of this problematic situation is a combination of power and fear:

> Masculine sexual identity is established through feeling superior to women we are close to and through establishing our sense of identity in a masculine competitive world. It is as if we only know how to feel good ourselves if we put others down. (Seidler, 1985, p. 169)

Traditional 'masculinity' focuses on dominance and independence, an orientation to the world which is active and assertive, which valorises competitiveness and turns its face from intimacy, achieving esteem in the glorification of force. The fear at the heart of this image is of emotion – that which makes us vulnerable and 'womanly'; emotion is dangerous not only because it implies dependence, but also because it is alien, a representation of all that masculinity rejects. This fear of emotion in turn makes sex both over- and underinvested in by men. Sex is one of the few socially acceptable ways in which men can aspire to closeness with others, and as such it becomes the carrier of all the unexpressed desires that men's emotional illiteracy produces. However, this same power of sex to produce emotionality makes it dangerous to men whose identity is built upon the rejection of emotion; sex then becomes split off, limited to the activity of the penis, an act rather than an encounter. It is also a means of taking up a particular place in the world of men: sexual 'conquest' as a symbol of male prowess. The link between such a form of masculinity and sexual abuse is apparent: it is not just present, but *inherent* in a mode of personality organisation that rejects intimacy. Sex as triumph and achievement slides naturally into sex as rejection and degradation of the other.

There is a number of different accounts of the processes which construct masculine sexuality along the lines described above, ranging from the sociobiological 'male sexual drive' discourse to radical feminist accounts that read masculine psychology as an organisation of force relations to oppress women. One informative approach derives from the object relations school of psychoanalysis, particularly as it has been re-worked by feminist theorists and practitioners such as Chodorow (1978) and Eichenbaum and Orbach (1982). These writers emphasise the negative impact of gender-differentiated child care on the ability of boy children to experience themselves as dependent and emotionally connected with others. As a defensive manoeuvre against his own emotional needs, reinforced by the cultural derogation of womanhood and the opposition between 'feminine' and 'masculine' qualities, the boy's ability to form intimate relationships is suppressed while his assertive, aggressive and spoiling elements are supported. Hence, 'successful' masculine socialisation involves effective action in the external world at the price of a fragile and underdeveloped emotional capacity, which fuels both an urgent demand for more closeness with the mother and a destructive rejection of her.

> The common product of this developmental process is an adult male whose capacity to nurture is severely impaired, whose ability to form affectionate relationships is restricted, and whose masculine identity, since it rests upon a repudiation of his identification with the person who first cared for him, is forever in doubt. (Herman, 1981, p. 56)

There is a number of difficulties with this version of the psychoanalytic theory of masculine development: for instance, it makes it unclear how some people come to rebel against their traditional gender role, and it concentrates so strongly on the mother–child bond that it neglects consideration of wider social processes (see Frosh, 1987a). It does one important thing, however, and that is to move discussion of the sources of sexual abuse away from specific traumatic events that occur almost accidentally to particular men, and towards those normative processes in socialisation that make sexual abuse possible. This is not to say that there may not be particular causes which create an abuser out of any particular man: the model provided by Finkelhor (1984) and quoted earlier supplies examples of just such causes, with the experience of having been abused oneself appearing as a highly significant predisposing event. Rather, the point here is that there are systematic features of masculine sexuality which contribute to sexual abuse; in some ways, it is the inhibition which non-abusive men demonstrate towards sex with children that has to be explained more than the acts of the others. There are many important differences between child sexual abuse and the rape of adult women, for instance connected with the proportion of abusers that are strangers (which is higher in rape), the repeated nature of child sexual abuse, or the amount of force employed. But there is also the significant link that both types of sexual exploitation involve the mixing of sex and dominance in a manner that reflects the confusion at the heart of masculine sexuality. This sexuality, the psychoanalytic account proposes, is not 'determined' to be this way through biological means. It is constructed as a child develops in a particular culture through the medium of exposure to specific individuals and common cultural norms. Dominance, gender, sex, abuse: these terms are separable, but they run together in our world to produce the conditions under which child sexual abuse can occur and be a common, everyday event.

The child seductress

It has been pointed out by many authors that men who sexually abuse children are particularly adept at rationalising their actions in terms of the provocations of their victims – the overwhelming seductive power of the children themselves. Occasionally, the language is that of the 'concerned parent' finding a particularly concrete way of educating his child; more often it is the language of the male sexual animal, unable to control his passion in the face of desire. Sometimes, the language is specifically that of humiliation, familiar to all men, and to all women as recipients: 'she asked for it'. Such rationalisations may appear extraordinary in the light of the realities of child sexual abuse ('poor man, brought down by the lust of that four-year-old'), but they are also reflected in a powerful array of contemporary representations, from the crude pornography of men's magazines to the more sophisticated pornography of some 'art' books and 'serious' literature. The child seductress is not, therefore, a desperate and self-serving invention of men who abuse children; it is a pervasive cultural image upon which these men draw. It thus links the actions of some men (who sexually abuse children) with the desires of millions of other men (who in fantasy do the same).

Given the pervasiveness of the fantasy of the child seductress, it is perhaps no surprise to discover that the professional literature on child sexual abuse – specifically on incest – has also shown a tendency to 'blame the victim'. Finklehor (1979) identifies two related groups of theories which have dominated the literature, both of them focusing on the attributes of children (girls and boys) that encourage their sexual victimisation. The first of these runs exactly parallel to the fantasies described above, although the explanation given for the child's behaviour is medicalised instead of located in their desires. It involves the proposal that some children whose needs are not met through conventional channels discover that they can obtain affection by arousing an adult sexually; they therefore approach adults in this way, actively seducing them. The second class of theories makes the child less active, but reads into the fact that incestuous liaisons are often prolonged the idea that children (perhaps because of disturbance) collude with them. Herman (1981) provides an example that incorporates both of these theories: she quotes a psychiatry textbook passage which informs students that

> The daughters collude in the incestuous liaison and play an active and even initiating role in establishing the pattern. The girls may be frightened and lonely and welcome their fathers' advances as expressions of paternal love. (Henderson, quoted in Herman, 1981, p. 40)

This is clearly distinct from the sexual provocateur image of pornography, but it is not far removed from the rationalisation that legitimises sexual abuse as somehow in the interests of the child: it supplies affection, the much-needed 'paternal love'. It also shifts the responsibility for the abuse, in the careful and sympathetic jargon of therapeutic discourse, from the man who exploits a child's need for love to the child who has the need. To be a victim, in this model, is at least to have colluded in being victimised, even if one has not created the situation in the first place.

In most recent critiques, Sigmund Freud is identified as prime culprit and originator of the professional tendency to discount sexual abuse or blame it on the victim. His fall from grace is held to have resided in the famous transition from a seduction theory of neurosis, which explained hysteria as the result of real childhood sexual victimisation, to the theory of fantasy, which reinterpreted patients' memories as wishes. This was in many respects a crucial reinterpretation of material, marking the real beginning of psychoanalysis as a discipline devoted to the mapping and explanation of subjective experience. But it also merged with cultural prescriptions to support the tendency among therapists to write off the accounts of sexual abuse given by victims. Instead of being recognised as referring to real events, in many cases resulting in trauma and long-term consequences, reports of sexual abuse were often read by psychoanalysts as wishes, incentuous desires mistaken for reality. Even if the genuineness of the abuse was impossible to ignore, it was commonly seen as provoked by the child – a spilling-over of unconscious desires into real life. In one sweep, psychoanalysis thus combined a tendency to cover up the existence of child sexual abuse with a reworking of the child seductress image, once again making the child the source of her own distress.

There is much justification for this assault on psychoanalysis, both in the specific instances of its neglect of child sexual abuse and its derogation of women, and in the general area of the subordination of real events beneath an overriding concern with fantasy (see Miller, 1984). It could also be the case that psychoanalysis has contributed to the abuse of child sex victims by supporting a climate in which their stories are ignored; this may well have made many victims more vulnerable to continued abuse, and would certainly have accentuated their feelings of guilt, distress and confusion as the world of supposedly therapeutic adults proves indifferent to, and rejecting of, their pleas for recognition.

Children's sexuality

Despite the valid criticisms of psychoanalysis presented above, it has made a significant contribution to work in the area of sexual abuse by developing a sophisticated account of the nature and origins of sexuality. For instance, the notion of infantile sexuality, however much it tends to confuse issues of what might be meant by 'sexual', importantly combats a romanticised image of childhood innocence which actually makes children more vulnerable by denying them access to sexual knowledge. In outline, psycho-analysis holds that children are sexual beings from the start of life, with desires that are articulated sensually. Observed behaviours such as sucking are interpreted as the expression of these internal sexual feelings in a way that makes them structurally similar to equivalent adult behaviours, however much more rudimentary their form might be. So, infants who are sucking intensely or 'aggressively' are understood to have feelings that mirror these actions, in this case oral aggressive desires. Similarly, the interest that many older toddlers show in faeces and the pleasure they apparently demonstrate in holding and letting go are interpreted not just as the expression of a form of intellectual interest in new phenomena and achievements, but more deeply as an expression of desires for pleasure that centre around the anal region. The famous Freudian progression operates in this way: children have sexual drives that are expressed through the bodily modes characteristic of early periods in development, beginning with the oral region (sucking, biting), moving to the anal area (defecating, soiling) and then to the phallic region (masturbatory activity). Following this, there is supposed to be a 'latency period' in which sexual desires withdraw while the child develops her or his social and cognitive skills; this phase comes to an end with puberty. In all this, the drives themselves remain essentially the same, simply developing more coherence and being expressed in progressively more adult ways.

In addition to the general notion that infantile sexuality exists and is represented in different modes of behaviour, Freudian psychoanalysis proposes that there are some universal developmental experiences which have a crucial structuring effect on sexuality, and on the mind in general. The most significant such experience, and one particularly relevant for the area of child sexual abuse, is that which goes under the name of the 'Oedipus complex'. Freud's idea is reasonably simple, at least as far as the sexual development of the boy is concerned. Sexuality consists of a core drive which is simply bent on pleasure, and which takes no particular person or thing as its object. Through experience, the child discovers that some objects provide more pleasure than others; not surprisingly, the mother is the best of these objects, as her activity is centred around the child. So the child's sexual desires becomes focused on the mother. At the phallic stage of development, this is reflected in a wish to displace the father and possess the mother sexually. However, translation of this wish into action is impossible because it would transgress the incest taboo; specifically, the child's desire for the mother is contradicted by paternal authority, which is fantasised by the child to mean the threat of castration. The child's obedience to this threat – that is, his terror within the 'castration complex' – results in his renouncing (repressing) his passion and identifying with the father. Importantly, in this account the incest taboo is *not* seen as natural, despite its apparent universality in one form or another; it is, in fact, incestuous desire that is natural, because it reflects the free play of the drives, operating without consideration of the conventions that determine what is or is not an acceptable sexual object. In fact, it is the universality of incestuous desire that creates the need for universal taboos. Ordinary male sexuality therefore results from a renunciation of other possible forms of sexuality; it is built on a repression of 'natural' incestuous feelings rather than being an expression of nature itself.

Given that it is girl children who are the primary victims of sexual abuse, and that it is they who are represented in the image of the 'child seductress', it is worth considering Freud's description of the origin of feminine sexuality. According to Freud, there is little divergence between male and female development until entry into the phallic phase, as children of both sexes are attached to the mother and both boys and girls experience similar oral and anal impulses. At the phallic stage, the centre of erotogenesis for the boy shifts from the anus to the penis, his desire becoming that of penetration and possession of the mother. The little girl, in contrast, is dependent on her clitoris for sexual stimulation and soon becomes aware of its inferiority as an organ, resulting in a mixture of damaging emotions: a general sense of her own inferiority in the world, her distance from power, a hateful rage at the mother for having created her like that, in her own image, and a passionate envy of the real thing, the penis possessed by father and brother alike. Thus, the castration complex – that is, her recognition of herself as already castrated – pushes the girl into the Oedipus situation, in which her desire is to displace the mother in order to get for herself a share in the father's power. Hence the virulent reproaches that Freud supposes young girls to feel against their mothers; hence also the change in sexual object from mother to father which is supposedly characteristic of femininity. Finally, the desire for the penis must itself be renounced and replaced by the desire for a baby, preferably a boy.

There are some significant consequences of this tale of female psychosexual development. In the case of the boy, the castration complex forces a tremendous repression of incestuous desire and a strong identification with the father, giving rise to the punitive and powerful internalised conscience, structured into what Freud calls the 'super-ego'. No such mechanism operates for girls: they are supposed to remain in the Oedipus situation for a relatively long time and leave it only incompletely and with difficulty. Consequently, the Oedipal romance is more durable and pervasive for girls: desire for the father may never be properly repressed. Secondly, passivity is encouraged in the girl: with her recognition of the inferiority of the clitoris she gives it up (at least as an object of masturbation – a claim that most feminists have challenged) and thus also gives up a more active stance towards her sexuality. As Mitchell (1974) puts it, the dominance of passivity enables a transition to occur 'from the active wanting of her mother to the passive aim of wanting to be wanted by the father' (p. 108), a classic formulation of what is supposed to be women's role and difficulty in intimate relations.

The Freudian formulation of children's sexuality has been given in detail above for two main reasons. First, it has exerted a powerful, even dominant, influence over conceptualisations of childhood sexuality used by researchers and also by therapists working closely with children of all kinds, including those who have been sexually abused. Secondly, it is the most detailed theory of sexuality in childhood that exists. Its major virtues are: that it is willing to recognise manifestations of sexuality even in very young children; that it explores the developmental path that sexuality takes as it matures rather than supposing that it simply appears, magically, during adolescence; that it is willing to deal seriously with children's fantasies, fears and emotions around sex; and that it locates all this in a searching interrogation of family life. For psychoanalysts, children are not asexual, nor is their sexuality fully formed, and it may well be that it is the transition from infantile behaviour and experience to a rich and free adult sexuality that is most marred by sexual abuse. In particular, given their ideas on the centrality and difficulty of incestuous desires in childhood, analytically inclined therapists have often been very clear in articulating the deleteriousness of adult–child sexual encounters, particularly for girls involved in liaisons with their fathers. In the psychoanalytic view, father–daughter incest is particularly harmful because it makes the Oedipal fantasies of the girl concrete and interferes with the progression of her development towards autonomy, a controlled selfhood, and relationships outside the family.

There are numerous criticisms that can be made of the Freudian view of childhood sexuality. Some of these come from within the psychoanalytic movement itself, especially from object relations theorists (see Frosh, 1987a, for a detailed account). These workers take issue with Freud's notion of a sexual drive and suggest that sex should better be understood as an expression of a desire for intimacy – a suitable vehicle in which the fundamental human drive towards fulfilling personal relations can be carried. In this logic, one of the harmful effects of child sexual abuse would be to split sex from its rightful place at the apex of good personal relations, making it instead a threatening and aggressive violation. Alternatively, the sexualisation of contacts with adults in childhood can be seen as introducing sex too early and too powerfully to the child, making the formation of relationships without sex impossible. These ideas are obviously very appealing, and object relations theory contributes substantially to our own understanding of how masculine sexuality can be constructed to become abusive, as described in the previous section. Feminist object relations theorists have also presented an account of feminine development which is distinctly superior to the confused and misogynistic Freudian theory (see Chodorow, 1978; Eichenbaum and Orbach, 1982). But object relations theorists – and, indeed, all post-Freudians – have had little to add to Freud's detailed description of the sexual stages, leaving them still as the major psychoanalytic theory in this area.

More criticisms have arisen from outside psychoanalysis, both in terms of the victim-blaming uses to which it can be put (crediting children with sexual desires can lead to regarding them as the instigators of adult–child sexual contacts, as described above) and in terms of its substance. Some of these latter criticisms are conceptual, particularly disputing Freud's notion that children's engagement in sensual behaviour is in some way equivalent to what is called 'sexuality' in adults. For example, Jackson (1982) argues that it makes no sense to call a behaviour 'sexual' if it does not have the subjective significance of 'sex' for the child, whatever its external form. She, like many other writers, would substitute the term 'sensual' here, in an attempt to clarify how actions which produce bodily pleasure only gradually come to accrue the meanings characteristic of sexuality. While it is correct to point out the cumulative nature of children's sexuality – it does not start fully formed – approaches such as that of Jackson create a range of new difficulties. One is the assumption that it is possible to articulate clearly the 'meaning' of sexuality; part of the Freudian argument is that this meaning is both fragmentary and disparate, including a host of variations in adults and a range of subjective re-organisations in children. The 'sensuality' approach also raises the difficult issue of determining when sexuality appears. The point that psychoanalysis makes is that sexuality has a history, and this history begins in childhood. Calling certain childhood experiences 'sexual' makes this link.

Children's sexual behaviour

Freud's account has also been challenged descriptively, on the grounds that its version of children's sexual interests is factually incorrect. Studies revealing the lack of universality of the Oedipus complex fall into this class, although there appears to be a dearth of literature on what normal childhood sexual behaviour is actually like. Rutter's (1983) review is still the most reliable source for material of this kind, even though it is based on work largely carried out in the 1950s and 1960s. In outline, the most important points made in this paper are as follows.

1. In the male infant, erections of the penis occur from birth, at a frequency of three to eleven times per day in the first few months. These may be unpleasant at first, and are certainly reflex in quality, but infants of both sexes soon begin to run and touch their genitals, along with other bodily parts. Gradually, genital manipulation gains an 'erotic' quality as it is found to be pleasurable. The rate of genital manipulation is quite high: Newson and Newson (1963) found 36 per cent of mothers of one-year-olds reported genital play in their children, with pulling the penis by boys much commoner than genital stimulation by girls. Orgasm-like responses have been observed as early as five months, but usually this occurs later.

2. Genital interest increases in the two- to five-year period. The study of middle-class American children by Sears *et al.* (1957) found that about half the boys were reported to indulge in sex

play or genital handling; the rates are probably lower in girls (about 16 per cent).

3. Games involving undressing or sexual exploration are common by age four, with a wide range of activities being shown by pre-schoolers. Rutter notes that, 'Exhibitionistic and voyeuristic activities with both other children and adults are characteristic, masturbation occurs, children attempt to fondle their mother's breasts, and it appears from the nature of their play that urination is associated in children's minds with sex activity' (p. 325).

4. There is *no* 'latency' period in the sense of a time in middle childhood when the frequency of sexual activity is reduced, although sexual behaviour may be more concealed. Sexual activity actually increases during this period: in boys, rates of masturbation rise from around 10 per cent at seven years to 80 per cent at thirteen; heterosexual play is shown by about a third of boys at age eight. The rates are lower for girls, but the rising pattern is the same. These findings are also supported by Goldman and Goldman's (1982) study of children's sexual thinking: although children show more inhibitions in talking about sexuality at this time, they also show increasing interest in, and knowledge of, sex.

5. Homosexual play in boys (which mostly consists of mutual handling of genitals) and girls shows a gradual rise during childhood, reaching 25 to 30 per cent at thirteen years.

Although this does not bear specifically on Freudian theory, it is worth noting that sexual experience among adolescents is fairly extensive, although perhaps not as extensive as is sometimes represented. Schofield (1965), whose survey was based upon a national random sample of English fifteen- to nineteen-year-olds, found that most teenagers had had their first serious contacts with the opposite sex between twelve and fourteen years, the girls earlier than the boys. Sixteen per cent of Schofield's sample were regarded as 'sexually experienced'. A later British study by Farrell (1978) suggests that rates increased in the 1970s: 51 per cent of sixteen- to nineteen-year-olds were sexually experienced; 12 per cent of girls and 31 per cent of boys were 'fully sexually experienced' by age sixteen. Other studies confirm the general trend of these findings (see Goldman and Goldman, 1982, for a brief review).

With the exception of findings on the latency period and, to a lesser extent, the Oedipus complex, the results of the studies summarised above generally support psychoanalytic views of the existence of infantile sexuality. It is less clear that sexual development occurs through the psychological stage progression postulated by Freud, and even less likely that his description of femininity is accurate, but it does seem that children learn the pleasurable possibilities of masturbation early on, and that the extent and sophistication of their sexual interests and knowledge accumulates throughout childhood. Children discover bodily pleasure and gradually learn the full extent of sexual meanings; they have fantasies about sexual acts, child-bearing and birth; they are active participants in their sexuality rather than innocents to be ignored or kept ignorant. None of this, however, changes one central fact about child sexual abuse. Over and over again, it has to be restated that child sexual abuse is a common phenomenon *in reality*, that the victims of child sexual abuse are *victims*, that children do not have the power to seduce grown men against their will, that children who are looking for affection are desiring precisely that, and are not 'in fact' asking for sex. Those children who do attempt to sexualise affectionate relationships do so as a learnt sequel to particular experiences, usually of being sexually abused. Whatever fantasies or wishes children might have, it is adults who decide whether they will be the objects of sexual encounters, for adults have power over children and can define and manipulate their desires as they wish.

3

A Family Affair?

In the previous chapter a model of child sexual abuse was outlined which emphasises the general significance of masculine sexuality and the general vulnerability of children. In addition, some specific contributory factors were also identified, notably experiences of abuse in the childhood of abusers themselves. The model also proposes an intermediate stage between the potentiality for abuse and its actual occurrence; this stage is most easily conceptualised as the overriding of certain inhibitions. In this chapter, we attempt to elaborate on the most important of these inhibitions in cases of *repeated* child sexual abuse, that is, abuse which is also surrounded by secrecy and by the failure of responsible adults either to perceive it or to take effective action to prevent its recurrence. In these cases the family is of crucial significance, whether or not the abuse is actually incestuous. In particular, given the circumstances under which most children are brought up in our society, the role of the child's mother is of great importance: repeated abuse means at least that a child has not been able to confide in her or his mother or that she has not been in a position to do anything about the abuse. In what follows, the currently dominant explanatory model of repeated child sexual abuse, the *family systems model*, is outlined and discussed in conjunction with descriptions of family life in abusive families. Later in the chapter we examine the position of mothers in cases of child sexual abuse. Most of the literature refers to intrafamilial abuse (incest), but has relevance for all repeated abuse.

Abusive families

Most descriptions of families in which sexual abuse occurs agree on the conventionality of these families – their rigid adherence to an almost stereotypical patriarchal structure, Herman (1981), for example, depicts the families of the female incest victims that she interviewed as 'conventional to a fault', the fathers being 'perfect patriarchs' (p. 71). In these families, and also in those where fathers were 'seductive' towards their daughters but had not actually abused them, sex roles were very traditional, with few mothers working outside the home and where 'male superiority was unquestioned', women being treated as having no real rights of their own. Fathers often dominated the households by the use of force (half the informants had seen their mothers beaten) and exerted very strict control over the activities of their womenfolk. Combined with the characteristic unavailability of the mothers in these families, this often meant that the daughters were placed in a very exposed position, under threat from powerful and demanding men who might also appear to be the only prospective source for the fulfilment of needs for affection.

This description of incestuous families as patriarchal-authoritarian combines in the literature with alternative, or perhaps complementary, accounts that focus on the weakness and neediness of all family members (including the fathers) and the fragility with which the family is held together. In some, the picture given is of emotionally dependent and weak men who are dominated by their wives, even if on the face of it the father has authority (e.g. Furniss, 1984). The men are then held to be likely to turn to their daughters as partners on an equivalent emotional level, especially if the wife is sexually rejecting.

Other theorists emphasise the importance of secrecy and insecurity in all family members. Perhaps because of real histories of abandonment in the lives of the parents and their children, maintaining the family together as a unit comes to take absolute priority, with the incest victim or victims sacrificing themselves to this end. Thus, according to this theory, the fragility of family relationships coupled with a deep fear of break-up results in replacement of the weak parental bond by an arrangement whereby the father is tied into the family by his incestuous link with his daughter. The secrecy and danger which inevitably surrounds incest then serves to cement the family together: danger of discovery leads to a strengthening of family defences and an extremely powerful taboo on speaking about and uncovering the incest. Family members' inability to communicate with one another is turned to good account here, becoming a way in which the family is kept together, everyone bound by the power of their dangerous secret. The association of child sexual abuse with conservative family values and sexual inhibition is consistent with family dynamics of this kind: secrecy, authoritarianism and emotional inarticulateness produce the precise conditions in which desperate measures will come to the fore.

A recent theory that attempts to integrate these observations of the secret life of abusive families is *family systems theory*. A representative account is that given by Furniss (1984), who argues that at the root of father–daughter incest is a dysfunctional family arrangement in which the parents suffer from 'emotio-sexual' problems that lead to inter-generational confusions, particularly surrounding dependency and sexuality. In addition, a family taboo on facing up to tensions produces the conditions under which these confusions turn into cross-generational sexual liaisons; the characteristic secrecy of such families is then enhanced, perpetuating the sexual abuse. The origin of incest is thus a parental conflict that becomes incorporated into a pervasive muddling and obscuring of family relationships serving the end of preserving the family against the pressures that threaten to smash it apart. Furniss' conclusion, from his analysis of forty-seven cases, is as follows:

> Despite different aetiological and precipitating factors, the underlying process in the relationships leading to the incest pattern was always the hidden emotio-sexual tension or conflict between the parents, who are locked in an unequal emotio-sexual partnership, and the distance in the mother–daughter relationship. The inability of the parents to deal with the specific confusion between their sexual and emotional problems and the introduction of a taboo against the acknowledgement of the tension and conflict in the family, sets the scene for the incest. (Furniss, 1984, p. 310)

The child functions both as parent and partner to the father, yet this structural incongruity is denied by all family members for fear that recognising it would signal the death of the family itself. Thus, family members are bound 'into a collusive system in which the incest can continue for many years' (Furniss, 1984, p. 310).

Furniss suggests that there are two distinct forms of family pathology that typically underpin incest; these are seen as the 'extremes of a continuum' rather than two distinct groups, as both fit the general scheme given above. The first form is *conflict avoidance.* In these families, marital estrangement – particularly sexual estrangement – threatens to produce family break-up; however, the individuals involved are too insecure to be able to cope with such an event, or even to recognise the reality of the family tension itself. Incest between father and daughter then arises as a more-or-less conscious delegation of the daughter to take over the wife's sexual role, removing a major source of stress and effectively binding the family together in the firm web of incestuous secrecy. No one acknowledges what is happening; the family's self-image and their presentation to the outside world is moral and idealised; the incest effectively removes the pressure from the marital relationship. The girl concerned is both victimised and central, distant from her mother but also essential to her. Fathers in such families are 'emotionally immature' and threatening; mothers are 'emotionally rigid' and 'over-moralistic', providing practical care but neglecting their daughters' emotional needs. If the incest is revealed it is usually denied; if undeniable the family is liable to collapse as its rigidly over-idealised self-image is destroyed.

The second type of family pattern that Furniss describes as typical of incest is *conflict regulation*. Families which show this pattern are far more openly 'disturbed' than conflict-avoiding families; they are disorganised and argumentative, frequently violent, with obviously weakened generational boundaries and role confusions. What they share with the other type of family is a terror of abandonment that leads them to aim to stay together even at great cost; the cost here is that of a daughter sacrificed to deflect the father's agression from his wife, and 'level off the peaks of the open marital conflict which threatens the homeostasis and cohesion of the family' (p. 307). In contrast to the secrecy that lies within the conflict-avoiding family, conflict regulators may be open about incest with one another, but hide it from the outside world.

> The collusion between the parents increases the father's dependence on his wife, and she, in turn, may even openly facilitiate the incest. this serves, despite all conflicts, to keep the father emotionally dependent and firmly bound to the family. (p. 307).

More than one child may be involved in this form of incest as boundaries collapse under the pressure of the father's emotional immaturity and the mother's deficiencies, The fact that the incest was already recognised within the family also means that it may not be affected by exposure to the outside world: disclosure may lead to a strengthening of family ties and, later, to a resumption of incest if the situation allows.

The essence of the family systems model, then, is the argument that incest derives from disturbances in family relationships, and that child sexual abuse can only be fully understood when it is located in the context of these disturbances. Evaluating this model is a complex problem. There is little empirical evidence enabling one to judge how frequently the relationship constellations described above actually characterise incestuous families. This means that, at best, the family systems approach can be seen as a hypothesis to govern research and to serve as a guide for clinical practice; its appeal may be as much due to the fashionableness of family therapy as to its intrinsic value. On the other hand, as the reports quoted throughout this chapter reveal, intrafamilial child sexual abuse does take place within a context of emotional deprivation and neglect and disturbances in family relationships which needs to be recognised and conceptualised if such abuse is to be fully understood. The family systems model at least allows one to begin this task. It also presents a reminder that child sexual abuse, as well as being a serious problem in its own right, may *also* be linked to, or indicative of, other problems in family and individual functioning. In addition, the family systems model tends to move the focus of analysis away from the internal individual pathology of the abuser and towards the network of family relationships which allows incest to occur and continue, and which also will probably be the actual environment in which the victim – and possibly the abuser – will continue to live. In focusing on family structure and here-and-now interactions, the family systems model, like family therapy in general, may offer more optimistic and immediately useful guidelines for action than those approaches that restrict themselves to the internal deficiencies of individuals.

There are, however, some telling criticisms that can be levelled against the family systems account. The poor empirical base of the theory has been mentioned above, but the same point can be made about alternative theories. A more specific criticism is that the family systems approach creates a false dichotomy between intra- and extrafamilial child sexual abuse. All its formulations are primarily concerned with incest rather than abuse by people outside the child's immediate family, even though most abuse is of the latter variety (albeit by people known to the child). This may be an unwarranted narrowing of focus, giving a spurious sense of reality to what may in fact be a description of a very small number of families. It may be, of course, that disorganised families of the kind described by Furniss put their children at greater risk for all forms of sexual abuse, however, this could be true of the conditions that lead to childhood difficulties in general rather than being a specific account of sexual abuse. Similarly, the family structures designated by Furniss as underlying incest are very much like those proposed by other family theorists as predisposing to other kinds of childhood emotional disturbance. In fact, the 'conflict-avoiding/conflict-regulating' dichotomy is probably the most popular of all descriptions of family pathology. In clinical practice, a far wider range of family types appears than that represented in Furniss's limited scheme. This suggests that while it may make some sense of the family background to incest, it cannot be seen either as predictive of, or specific to, child sexual abuse.

Other criticisms of the family systems model are more conceptual. It is an approach that tends to implicate women in partial responsibility for the sexual abuse of their children, despite its affiliation to relationship concepts rather than individualistic ones. For example, in the CIBA (1984) version of Furniss's account, the characteristics of incestuous families are given mostly in terms of the mothers – emotionally distant in conflict-avoiding families, practically and emotionally deficient in conflict-regulating ones (p. 12). More subtly, mothers and fathers – and perhaps even other siblings – are put on an equivalent level in the construction of sexual abuse, as it is made into the product of a certain pattern of family relationships rather than as something that arises from any one individual.

In Chapter 2, it was argued that there is an inherent link between child sexual abuse and the organisation of masculine sexuality; the family systems model continues a long line of theories which deny this link and instead attempt to dissipate the responsibility for abuse among a number of people. A defence of the family systems model might be that it does not attempt to provide a causal account at all, merely a description of the typical relationships which surround incest. However, this is at odds with much of the language of family theorists ('the constellation that brings about incest.' – CIBA, 1984, p. 13; 'the key factor which brings about incest.' – Furniss, 1984, p. 303); it also begs the question of what *does* cause child sexual abuse to occur, and why the family model does not deal with it.

Finally, there is another questionable assumption in the family systems model of child sexual abuse: the implication that there is something about such families that has gone wrong, that is qualitatively distinct from 'normal', healthy families. However, just as men who abuse children seem to be demonstrating in an extreme way patterns of desire and behaviour which are present in all men, so families in which children are sexually abused may be dramatising an aspect of family life that is inherent in conventional family structure. Patriarchy is partially defined by the dominance of men as *owners* of women and children; less theoretically, the ethos of privacy and possessiveness that surrounds the family holds the seeds of sexual exploitation just as it holds the promise of more acceptable tendencies such as protection and care. It may be a fine point to decide which tendency wins out in most families: the frequency with which families break up, and with which women and children are physically as well as sexually abused, suggests that the destructive element in family life may be very powerful. The point here, however, is not to launch a full-scale attack on families, only to note that a theory of sexual abuse that is founded on the notion of family dysfunction not only awaits proper validation, but also may miss broader factors that make sexual abuse a possibility in all families, however 'normal' they may be.

Mothering

It is not only family systems theorists who see the behaviour and position of the mothers of sexually abused children as a crucial element in the development and perpetuation of the abuse. Although many writers are cautious about this, suggesting that maternal 'failure' is only one element in causation, there are many examples of occasions on which the role of the mother is viewed as the primary source of sexual abuse. Sometimes this arises apparently unintended in the context of a more sophisticated account: for example, the CIBA (1984) report adheres to a family systems model of abuse, yet allows the following piece of linear thinking to slip through.

> When a mother withdraws from her family, her children and husband may turn to one another for support, practical assistance or comfort and

the foundations of an incestuous relationship are laid. In other cases a man deprived of his conjugal rights may turn to the nearest available source of gratification – a dependent child. (p. 9)

Although this passage contains an element of caution ('may'), its strong implication is that the withdrawal or sexual refusal of the mother is the *cause* of incest – it lays its 'foundations'. The language of 'conjugal rights' is particularly notable in this context. Presumably a wife has no 'right' to deny her husband sex if it is after all his 'right'; such unreasonable behaviour may thus legitimate his turning to another person over whom he has 'rights' – his daughter. This juxtaposition reveals the link that exists between attitudes towards, and abuse of, women and children: within the family, both are traditionally the property of the man.

Ward (1984) documents a number of passages from a variety of authors in which mother-blaming is transparent. To give just one example, Justice and Justice (1979) portray many mothers of abused childred as 'frigid' and wanting no sex with their husbands. To these authors, such behaviour on the part of a woman fits into the 'denial of conjugal rights' category: 'This is another way of bowing out of her role as a wife and giving reason to the husband to look elsewhere for sex . . . the mother feels relief when the daughter substitutes for her' (p. 79). Renvoize (1982), who is on the whole a more sympathetic observer of incest victims, also stresses the way the 'withdrawal' of the mother from family life produces a role reversal whereby the daughter substitutes for her; this combination of withdrawal and role reversal 'of course brings the father and daughter closer, encouraging the emergence of a dangerous relationship' (p. 105). As Ward (1984) shows, almost any behaviour on the part of the mother can be interpreted as contributing to, or perhaps causing, the abuse. She either passively colludes with the situation or actively abandons her child; she always knows what is happening yet never takes action; she both provokes the abuse by ignoring her husband and maintains it by failing to protect the child. Finally, there is the theory that mothers 'sacrifice' their daughters – either to get away from their husbands or to keep them committed to the family.

In the same way as the tendency to blame the victim (described in Chapter 2) diverts attention from the 'normal' psychopathology of masculine sexuality, so locating the origin of sexual abuse in the behaviour of mothers who are not fulfilling their roles produces a reading of abuse as a product of specific breakdowns in the smooth functioning of families rather than as an intrinsic element in family life itself. Two common assumptions are observable here. The first is that child sexual abuse does not accur in 'healthy' families; hence, if there is abuse, there must be a distortion present in the way the family operates. As described above, this is an assumption particularly central to the family systems view of abuse, but it is implicit in many other approaches. The second assumption, generally left unstated but frequently obvious, is that it is the role of women to create stability in family life, to maintain the health of the family system. Hence, if the system becomes disturbed and abusive, the woman must have abandoned her role. The extent to which these assumptions can be upheld is questionable. In the discussion in Chapter 2, we moved from the notion that abusive men have particular disturbances, to the idea that sexual abuse is a potential within all men, constructed as intrinsic to masculine sexuality. A possibility that must be considered here is that abuse is not a signal of pathological activity within an otherwise healthy 'institution', but that there are elements in *all* families that are potentially abusive – that it is something inherent in families themselves. The importance of this argument is that it directs attention away from a pathological group and instead requires us all to interrogate the abusive possibilities within us – as individuals and as family members. Abuse then ceases to be a foreign phenomenon; it is disturbingly familiar just as it is disturbingly common.

The argument presented above should not be taken to mean that there is no difference between a family in which abuse occurs and one in which it does not. If it is correct that the *potential* for abuse resides in all families and all men, then what differentiates the two groups of families is the power of inhibitory factors. The most important of these may well be the behaviour of the mother, but this is not the same as making the mother responsible for the abuse, still less the 'cause' of it. Put more formally, a full understanding of repeated child sexual abuse requires knowledge of the processes that invalidate the mother and others as protectors of the child. Read like this, there is a considerable amount of relevant evidence (mostly anecdotal, however) that mother–daughter relations in incestuous families are often poor, and that this contributes to the difficulty that children have in breaking out of the abusive bind.

Finkelhor (1984) found in his examination of the questionnaire protocols of his student sample that having an absent or ill mother was an important predictor of the likelihood of sexual abuse. This was also a strikingly consistent finding in Herman's (1981) interviews with forty women who had been the victims of incest: more than half of her informants remembered that their mothers 'had had periods of disabling illness which resulted in frequent hospitalisations or in the mother's living as an invalid at home' (p. 77). Thirty-eight per cent of the daughters had been separated from their mothers at some time during childhood either because their mothers were hospitalised or because they felt they could not cope with looking after their children. Depression, alcoholism and psychosis were among the most common problems that these mothers had, 'mysterious ailments which made them seem withdrawn, peculiar and unavailable'. It is also clear that many, perhaps most, sexually abused girls experience their mothers as distant and rejecting, and certainly remember their unresponsiveness to attempted communications concerning the abuse itself. In Finkelhor's (1984) study, the second most powerful predictor of abuse (after having a step-father) was having a mother who was punitive about sexual matters. It is a clinical impression reported by many writers that mothers often deny knowledge of the abuse even when its seems clear that they must have known it was occurring; whether this impression is accurate or not, it does seem to be shared by the daughters. For example, Herman (1981) notes about the women in her sample that, 'Many daughters believed that their mothers knew, or should have known, about the incest, and they bitterly resented the fact that their mothers did not intervene' (pp. 88–9), However, only a minority of the girls actually told their mothers (or anyone else) of the incest while they remained at home, and most of those who did were disappointed in the response.

> Most of the mothers, even when made aware of the situation, were unwilling or unable to defend their daughters. They were too frightened or too dependent upon their husbands to risk a confrontation. . . . They made it clear to their daughters that their fathers came first and that, if necessary, the daughters would have to be sacrificed. (Herman, 1981, p. 89)

In line with the general picture of mothers given earlier, Herman's sample of women who had grown up with 'seductive' but not overtly abusive fathers reported that they too had experienced bad relationships with rejecting and unsupportive mothers, but that their mothers had been less passive and isolated and more competent and healthy than those in the incestuous group. Perhaps because they were more firmly present in the family and stronger as individuals – more able to protect themselves – these women somehow managed to protect their daughters from abuse.

The consequences of the difficult mother–daughter relationships characteristic of families in which sexual abuse has occurred can be severe. The simplest way of describing these relationships is 'alienated': the distance that exists between mother and daughter in childhood and that is reflected in the mother's inability to recognise or prevent the abuse, continues in a hardened form into adulthood, with consequences for the daughter's ability to form fulfilling relationships throughout her life. Sexually abused girls often seem to blame their mothers for what has been done to them. For example, in Tsai and Wagner's (1978) sample of fifty sexually abused women, the thirty-one who had been abused by their fathers or step-fathers expressed at least as much anger towards their mothers as towards the abuser. Herman (1981) notes that many of the women in her sample became drawn into a competitive relationship with their mothers which centred on an alliance with the abusive father. As children, these women experienced their mothers as absent or rejecting, unable to provide the nurture and affection that they required. They perceived their fathers as experiencing the same insufficiencies of care; they also sometimes treasured the 'special relationship' that formed between them and their fathers, using it partly to hit back at their mothers, partly as the only available way to obtain something resembling affection. Their attitudes to their mothers was frequently hostile and disparaging, a mixture of anger, guilt and neediness.

> Though many could see that their mothers were ill or overwhelmed with their own problems, few, as children, could afford the luxury of compassion. They knew only that they bore the burden of their mothers' shortcomings and were obliged to nurture others while their own longings for nurture went unsatisfied. (Herman, 1981, p. 82)

The results of this process can only be speculated upon, but it seems likely that the derogation of mothers that comes to be an integral aspect of the family constellation surrounding incest will be internalised by daughters and will harmfully influence their own sense of themselves as women. What is being learnt by these girls is that women are objects of hostility and competition, not to be trusted, while men, who are abusive, demanding and inconsistently affectionate, validate a woman's existence when they select her as a sexual partner. At a deeper level, psychologically, incest victims may be harbouring unmet needs of an extremely powerful kind: fundamental desires for care and emotional support will have to be repressed in the face of the distance of the mother and the manipulation of these desires by the father. What the testimony of many incest victims suggests is that the absence of adequate parenting may be lamented even more strongly than the abusive attention that replaces it.

It may be that some of the observed intergenerational continuities in child sexual abuse can be explained by the processes described above. It is an apparent puzzle that there is a strong link between having been abused oneself in childhood and having children who are themselves sexually abused. The puzzle here is that the statistical link passes down a maternal chain (girls who are abused have daughters who are abused) and yet it is men who actually do the abusing. (Some of these men will themselves have been abused in childhood, but this still does not explain the maternal link.) There are various possibilities here. At the simplest level, many abused girls are desperate to get away from home, and consequently make themselves available to the first man who comes along – who may well be disposed to continuing the abusive chain. They may also retain an affection for their fathers and remain in contact with them, which might later on put their own children at risk; it is by no means uncommon for a man to abuse both his children and his children's children. Again, the confusion between affection and sexual activity often experienced by children who have been sexually abused makes them prime targets for sexually exploitive men later in life. With an internal self-image in which guilt, blame, anger and a sense of worthlessness combine, and with an experience in which dependency needs are met with rejection or sexual exploitation, victims of sexual abuse may fall prey to men who might go on to abuse their children. These women are also least likely to be able to prevent the abuse. Their history is such that mother–daughter relationships may be experienced as competitive and ambivalently hostile; their own unmet needs may be so profound and their self-esteem so low that the appropriately intense demands of their children (especially their daughters, with whom they are more likely to identify) provoke anxiety and rejection.

Finally, recognition of the fact that one's own child is being sexually abused is a traumatic and difficult process for anyone; how much more this is the case for women who have themselves been abused, for it is likely to bring back the despair and shame from their own childhood. It is perhaps not surprising, then, that the destructive family pattern surrounding sexual abuse may carry on into the next generation.

There are one or two clarifying points to be made here. The representation of mothers as causal agents in abuse was contested earlier, and this may seem to contradict the later account of the frequency with which breakdowns in mother–daughter relationships occur. In fact, there is no real contradiction here. Ward (1984) characteristically puts the equation at its most provocative: 'Even if a Daughter does experience her Mother as rejecting, neither she nor the Mother are asking for the Father to rape her' (p. 174). The experience of relationship breakdown and sexual abuse are not the same thing: the former may mean that abuse is less likely to be discovered or prevented, but the preconditions for sexual abuse have still to be present – and these, as discussed in the previous chapter, have their source in masculine, not feminine, psychology. In addition, the failure of mothers to protect their children is, at least in part, produced by some of the same factors which give rise to the abuse itself. These include the dominance of men in families which is in large part legitimised by an ideological stance that makes women and children into property. The common experience that women have of male violence and the economic dependence that characterises family life also militate against effective action being taken by mothers against abusive men. Again, the criminal law provides no guarantee that action taken by mothers will actually protect them or their children from further abuse – the consistent failure to prosecute abusers is a clear example of this. Mothers, particularly if they have been abused themselves, may also fear that they will be blamed for allowing the abuse of their children to happen, a fear confirmed by some of the professional literature. Finally, it ill behoves mental health professionals to criticise mothers for not believing or knowing how to respond to indications that their children are being sexually abused, when the sensitivity of professionals to these events is so newly, and precariously established. The women have very much more to lose.

Conclusion

In these three chapters some basic descriptors of child sexual abuse have been produced and various approaches towards understanding the causes of abuse have been discussed. We have emphasised the factors inherent in masculine sexuality and in the position of children that always make sexual abuse a possibility. We have criticised approaches which place the responsibility for abuse with children or with their mothers, but we have also drawn attention to the general breakdown in family relationships and the failure of inhibiting mechanisms that accompany repeated abuse. Our model is thus one in which a man with a predisposition to abuse (because of his personal history linked to general elements in masculine sexuality and social mores) has access to a child who is not adequately protected against him, for a variety of reasons. If abuse occurs and an effective screen of secrecy is placed over it, abusive acts may well be repeated unless inhibiting factors can be mobilised, with the role of the child's mother being of particular importance here.

In any specific case, this model distinguishes between (a) retrospective *explanation* of the relationships which surrounded the abuse, and (b) *responsibility* for the abuse, which clearly rests with the abuser, even though (particularly from the child's point of view) there may be a role for the mother or other carers in failing to protect the child. Each single incidence of child sexual abuse occurs within a particular context of impoverished or threatening personal relations, and in a general context of exploitative elements in masculine sexuality and of social subjugation of women and children.

The theoretical issues discussed in Part I are important for understanding child sexual abuse and for beginning the work of providing guidelines for intervention and therapy. In Part II, we spell out these guidelines, emphasising practical procedures.

Part II

Therapeutic Practice

4

Suspicion and Disclosure: Initial Professional Responses

Child sexual abuse characteristically faces social workers with a crisis, in which either a child has disclosed the existence of abuse, or an adult is expressing anxiety over what she or he perceives as suspicious signs. In this chapter, this crisis is placed in a statutory, relational/emotional and temporal context. We define the aims of intervention, consider some basic emotional and relational issues, describe the pathways leading to disclosure, and provide guidelines for interpreting suspicions and alerting signs. In Chapter 5, we go on to describe the information-gathering and assessment process, including details of the disclosure or elaboration interview, medical examination, initial family assessment and case conference.

The statutory framework

Figures 4.1 and 4.2 present a schematic view of the context of child sexual abuse and its professional management. They show the various stages of the occurrence, discovery and treatment of child sexual abuse, alongside a representation of the interlocking nature of child and family and professional 'systems'. Framing these events and relationships is the law, usually implemented according to locally agreed Area Review Committee guidelines. Although these guidelines vary from place to place, the statutory responsibilities of social services departments have a profound influence on the way all local authority social workers deal with child sexual abuse. The prime duty of social workers is to act to protect children, and to this

53

end they have available a number of legal options when they consider a child to be at risk, including the power to request removal of a child from her home. The difficulty facing social workers, and social services departments in general, when there is concern about a child's welfare is to balance the relative merits of immediate removal of that child (on a Place of Safety Order) against a slower and more planned approach. On the one hand, the danger of abuse and, ultimately, the immediate threat to a child's life, may be compelling reasons for action. On the other hand, the sudden removal of a child may in itself be a traumatic experience, and may guarantee neither the child's long-term safety nor emotional welfare. Place of Safety Orders are temporary measures which can only be extended through interim care orders or through Wardship proceedings. Extensive experience has shown that in cases of child sexual abuse, the less information is available at the time of obtaining the Place of Safety Order, the more difficult is the task of extending legal protection for the child, because of insufficient evidence. This may result in a child's return home, possibly to further abuse, because the original removal was poorly planned.

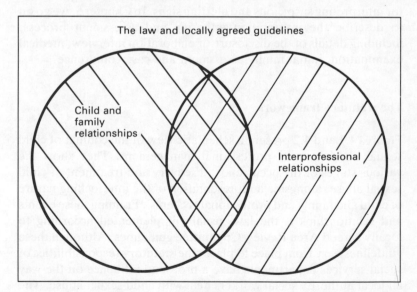

Figure 4.1 *Schematic representation of contexts of child sexual abuse*

Child sexual abuse presents exceptionally severe problems for social workers attempting to fulfil their protective duty. Except in cases of physical trauma, the secrecy and confusion surrounding child sexual abuse makes the collection of clear evidence a difficult and subtle process; in addition, careful assessment of the child's relationship context is necessary before decisions can be made about the appropriate protective steps. Careful interprofessional planning is almost always more effective than immediate, crisis-

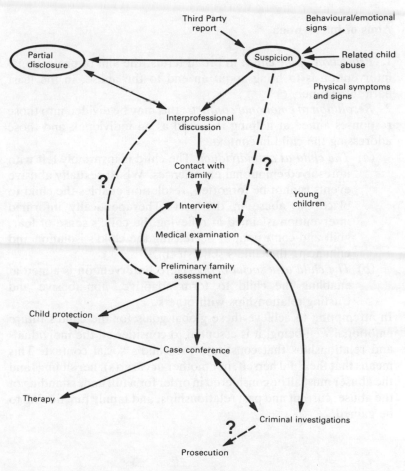

Figure 4.2

driven intervention. Although this places strain on social workers having to 'carry' the awareness of possible further abuse occurring while investigations are going on, the prospects of successful action with the least harmful impact on the child are greatly increased by this course of action. This is what is meant by 'therapeutic' professional practice; it is also the approach most likely to produce clear information and evidence on which child-care decisions can be made. It is upon these principles that the guidelines presented here are based.

Aims of intervention

1. *Protection of the child*: in broad terms, the aim of professional intervention is to bring about an end to the abuse, in the least harmful manner.
2. *Resolution of emotional conflicts*: this may be divided into those responses aimed at helping the child as an individual, and those addressing the child in context.

   (*a*) *The child as an individual.* The child is invariably left with unresolved emotional experiences. Whilst sexually abusive events cannot be forgotten, resolution enables the child to place the abuse in the past. Therapeutically informed intervention is aimed at relieving the child's sense of fear, guilt and confusion, at decreasing the child's isolation and enhancing the child's self esteem.

   (*b*) *The child as a social being.* Here, intervention is aimed at enabling the child to form adaptive, non-abusive and trusting relationships with others.

In attempting to achieve these global goals for the child's future emotional well-being, it is essential to consider all the individuals and relationships that constitute the child's social context. This means that the child herself, her mother or carer(s), her siblings and the abuser must all be considered in order for a full understanding of the abuse, current and past relationships, and family functioning to be gained.

Some emotional and relational issues

Inhibitions to disclosure

The many factors that can stand in the way of the recognition and disclosure process may be broadly divided into two groups: those that result from anxieties or concerns felt by the people who are in a position to recognise suspicions and receive the child's disclosure (called here 'professional inhibitions'), and those that arise in the child's network from the web of secrecy that always surrounds repeated sexual abuse.

Professional inhibitions

These vary, often closely paralleling the inhibitions experienced by the child and her family.

Professionals may believe that the consequences of intervention will be worse than those of the abuse itself. In fact, retrospective studies have clearly shown that a majority of adults who were repeatedly sexually abused as children but did *not* disclose the fact, have suffered adversely as a consequence. It also seems that those victims who have a relatively 'good' outcome in adult life are more likely to have found someone sympathetic and trustworthy in whom to confide (see Chapter 1). Current interventions await long-term evaluation, but despite awareness that incompetent or incomplete intervention may cause further harm, it is now considered unethical not to intervene.

Many professionals continue to harbour inhibitions privately when faced with intimate, often disturbing or unpalatable sexual details, especially involving young children. These inhibitions may arise from unresolved feelings about our own sexuality or sexual relationships or may reawaken memories of personally experienced abuse. Detailed accounts of sexual experiences may also evoke sexual excitement in the professional. The violation of presumed innocence is often particularly disturbing, and there is a clear need for opportunities to express one's feelings and reactions.

There may be doubts about the truthfulness of the accounts of the abuse. Children rarely allege abuse falsely, although there are situations in which a child may be used in a conflictual relationship by being induced to claim non-existent sexual abuse. Very occasionally, in an attempt to free themselves from difficult situations older adolescents claim to have been sexually abused. Professionals may fear the prospect of having to pass judgement on the truth or falseness of disclosed abuse. Whilst it is clearly in the interests of both the child and the abuser for the truth to be established, this is not always possible. However, it is very likely that, either way, there exists a serious problem, which merits professional involvement.

Uncertainty is sometimes felt about what constitutes acceptable touch between parents or adults and children at various ages, developmental stages and in different cultures. Misgivings about unecessarily pejorative labelling of normal affection may lead to reluctance in pursuing possible sexual abuse of a child. Consideration of the respective ages of the possible abuser and child, recourse to operational definitions and interprofessional consultation may all be helpful here.

The rights of children, as accepted by society, are more easily considered in theory than when a seemingly attached and valued child in an apparently well-functioning family is suspected of being sexually abused. In fact, the child sexual abuse may be a central component in maintaining the family's functioning.

A professional, such as a general practitioner, therapist or social worker, may feel dual and conflicting loyalties to the child and abuser, if both were previously known, or if the abuser was the patient or client. The 'best interests of the child' are here of paramount importance, and it may be helpful to involve a professional colleague in order to preserve a therapeutic relationship.

Feelings of anger or outrage may stand in the way of a clear professional response. Sharing one's feelings within a team is often very helpful.

Finally, uncertainty about procedure, fears of being unsupported within one's agency or by peers and colleagues, or lack of trust in other agencies, are not uncommon. There is often a sense of impending loss of control over a process once it has been initiated. A clear plan of action, based on established local procedures which include, as a prerequisite, a good working relationship between all the local professional agencies, is likely to alleviate some of the doubts and reservations which inhibit effective intervention.

The secret

At the time of disclosure, the intensity of the wish for secrecy to be breached and the abuse to be stopped will vary both within and between the individuals involved in the abuse and other family members. Furthermore, the degree to which different family members are aware of the sexual relationship and its abusive nature, varies. The only person who can be assumed to be aware of both the existence and nature of the sexual abuse is the abuser. (In very exceptional circumstances the abuser may be suffering from a psychotic illness or mental handicap sufficient to reduce his social awareness.)

Very young children may not be aware that the sexual contact imposed on them is abusive or wrong. This awareness, however, emerges as soon as an injunction to secrecy is presented to the child by the abuser, and it is likely to be conveyed by the child to anyone in whom she may confide. Based on their previous experiences, some children anticipate disbelief at disclosure. The child often fears the public declaration of what she perceives as her guilt in complying with the sexual relationship, particularly when, as children sometimes describe, pleasure has been gained from the sexual abuse. This dreaded public declaration may take the form of repeated interviews by the police and social workers and the giving of evidence in court. Some girls may fear the intrusion of a medical examination. Anticipation of punishment by the abuser or blame and rejection by the family, possibly leading to reception into care, are fears often expressed by sexually abused children at the time of disclosure.

Disclosure is usually regarded as betrayal of the abuser and is then recognised as the first step towards his incrimination. This is particularly painful for those children who feel some affection towards their abuser. Ambivalence of this kind often places the child in a personal predicament, realising that disclosure may mean termination of contact with a loved person as may ensue, for instance, if abuse was by a divorced father during access visits. Other children in the family who may be aware of the abuse will often not disclose for similar reasons.

The mother may or may not be aware of the existence of the abuse, whether within the family or outside. Having become aware of it, her position is particularly difficult. As the child's care-giver she is often forced into making a choice between her relationship with the abuser and the child. She may also be dependent on or intimidated by the abuser.

Abusers themselves are least likely to disclose the abuse, although those who are able openly to assume responsibility may well experience relief.

When sexual abuse occurs within a family, there will usually be strong pressure to keep it a secret from the outside world. The degree of organisation, maintenance of personal and intergenerational boundaries and openness of communcation within the family all determine how open the secret will be and how strong will be the injunction against letting it be known to outsiders. Threats and exhortations to secrecy may contribute to a child feeling too guilty or frightened to 'admit' to the existence of the sexual contact. However, the secrecy which is characteristic of intrafamilial child sexual abuse may also be found in cases where the abuser is not a family member. To the extent to which awareness of the abuse exists in the child's family, maintenance of the secret is related directly to the closeness of the relationship between the abuser and the child's care-giver. The closer that relationship, as when the abuser is a family friend or relative, the greater will be the degree of secrecy. The ultimate and most harmful form of this closeness comes when care-giver and abuser are the same person.

Thus, considerable variation is found between the status of different families and the feelings experienced by those involved in the sexual abuse. At the point of first encounter by a social worker or other professional with the abusing system, it is vital to be aware of the range of possible feelings which may be relevant to any child or family, and to retain an attentive and sensitive ear to the experience and emotions alive in this particular family, without prejudice.

Assault by a stranger

This form of abuse is likely to be sexually, physically and emotionally traumatic to the child, but may present problems of a different nature. There may be greater use of force, with physical traumatisation and overwhelming intimidation of the child. The child is likely to be acutely emotionally shocked and may not be in a fit state to give an immediate and detailed account of what happened. She is, however, unlikely to want, or indeed be able, to keep the assault a secret. Stranger-assault following the luring of a child, and which is not physically traumatic or grossly intimidating, may cause a child to feel guilty about having disobeyed instructions 'not to go with strangers', leading to a reluctance to talk about what happened.

Modes of presentation and recognition

Disclosure constitutes a critical and complex phase in the process of dealing with child sexual abuse, and there are many routes leading to it. Essentially, a new interface is formed between the family and the professional network, often social services. It constitutes a crisis for the former and it activates the latter. Whilst the crisis is undoubtedly traumatic, its precipitation offers a more hopeful prospect for real change.

As illustrated in Figure 4.2, recognition of abuse may follow either *suspicion* based on the child's circumstances, behaviour or physical symptoms or signs, or an actual *statement* by the child, indicating that abuse has occurred. In the latter case, it is assumed that the child is telling the truth. In cases of suspicion it is important to allow time for planning the intervention and the response to the crisis which will consequently be precipitated in the family. The more active the disclosure by the child or family, the less prepared a social worker is likely to be and yet the more quickly she or he will have to act. Conversely, when suspicion first becomes articulated within the professional network, there is nearly always time to plan the communication of this suspicion to the family and to prepare for the crisis which will ensue.

Following the initial contact between the child and family and social services, one of three outcomes will follow:

1. The abuse will be recognised and child protective, therapeutic and possibly criminal proceedings will be initiated.
2. Uncertainty will remain.
3. A decision will be made that no sexual abuse has taken place, following false allegations or the misinterpretation of phenomena.

Below we first discuss *suspicion* and its management. The chapter then deals with the routes taken by direct, though generally only partial, *disclosures*.

Suspicion: the route to disclosure or the discomfort of uncertainty?

With increasing public and professional awareness of child sexual abuse, more clues are being sought and more suggestive signs recognised. More children are thus being suspected of having been abused. For some children, the suspicions will be shown to be founded on evidence acceptable on the balance of probabilities or beyond reasonable doubt. In other cases, uncertainty is unresolved, and since the child protective measures cannot be undertaken lightly, the unresolved suspicion must sometimes uncomfortably remain. Nevertheless, it is always important to pursue suspicions: sensitive early detection of child sexual abuse, leading to effective protection and appropriate therapeutic response, offers the best hope for a positive long-term outcome for the child and family.

The child: suspicion of sexual abuse may arise from observations of a child's behaviour and indirect comments, or of physical symptoms or signs. Some of these are highly suggestive, while others are only compatible with (not diagnostic of) a sexually abusive causation.

The family: from a different perspective, it is recognised that certain family constellations and relationship patterns are commonly associated with the occurrence of child sexual abuse. The index of suspicion might, therefore, be raised when those relationship patterns are encountered. Attention here could conceivably constitute true primary prevention, since abuse may not yet have occurred.

Arousal of suspicion: the symptoms and signs of child sexual abuse

Child sexual abuse may lead to physical and behavioural sequelae, which are the outward manifestations of the abuse. Those outcomes about which the child is aware and which may indeed cause discomfort and lead to seeking medical or other help, are termed symptoms. Signs are those manifestations which are observed by others.

Table 4.1 lists a number of common signs and symptoms of child sexual abuse, divided into three aspects: physical manifestations, emotional and behavioural responses, and family relationship patterns. The following symbols are used in the table:

sy = symptom; si = sign;

* = highly suggestive of child sexual abuse (lack of * denotes a non-specific, but possible alerting sign);

(*) = a learnt pattern.

Table 4.1 Signs and symptoms of child sexual abuse

Aspect of abuse	Physical manifestations
1. *Trauma*	Vulvovaginal soreness or discomfort (*sy, si*)
	* Vaginal bleeding in pre-pubertal girls (*sy*)
	* Genital laceration (*si*)
	* Bruising in genital area (*si*)
	* Enlarged vaginal opening, scarred hymen (*si*)
	* Vaginal discharge (*sy, si*)
	Lax or pouting anal sphincter, anal fissures or scars (*si*)
	Rectal bleeding (*sy*)
	Faecal soiling or retention (*sy*)
	Discomfort on micturition and recurrent urinary tract infections (*sy, si*)
	Evidence of child abuse (*si*)
2. *Infection*	* Sexually transmitted disease, including genital warts (*sy, si*)
	Vaginal discharge (*sy*)
3. *Sexual intercourse*	* Pregnancy (particularly when identity of father is uncertain) (*sy, si*)

Emotional and behavioural manifestations

1. *Premature sexualisation*	(*)Explicit or frequent sexual preoccupation in talk and play (*si*)
	* Sexualisation of relationships (*si*)
	(*)'Premature' sexual awareness (*si*)
	* Undue avoidance of men (*si*)
	Masturbation (*si*)
2. *Experiences of guilt, confusion, anxiety, fear anger*	* Hints of possession of secrets (*sy*)
	* Running away from home (*sy*)
	* Parasuicide (*sy*)
	Child psychiatric problems (*sy, si*)
	Learning difficulties (*si*)

Family relationship patterns

Distant mother–child relationship
Parentified child
Parental conflict
Unclear intergenerational boundaries
Child abuse
Alcohol abuse

Notes on some of the manifestations

Vaginal discharge. The status of vaginal discharge is unclear, and further research is awaited concerning its true incidence, which appears to be common. Causes include infection and the presence of foreign bodies in the vagina. Both these could be a part or result of sexual abuse.

Sexualised play and 'premature' sexual awareness. Sexual exploration of one's own and other children's bodies is a part of normal childhood activity. This includes touching and mutual masturbation. It is difficult to define precisely those aspects of sexual play which arouse suspicion. Quantitatively, sexualised play which is a frequent preoccupation of a child, to the exclusion of other play, may well bring the child to the notice of carers. There may be a compulsive quality to the preoccupation, which might include coercion of another child, such as repeated pulling down of other children's pants. The content of the sexual play may also invite attention by its explicit adult sexual nature, such as attempted vaginal or anal intercourse and oral-genital contact. Such explicit play, or other display of unusual sexual knowledge or awareness, is very likely to be learnt, either from repeated or close witnessing of full adult sexual activity in the flesh, on video films or in books. It is, however, often a result of a child's own experiences of abuse.

The state of current knowledge is insufficient to distinguish confidently between these different learning situations. However, a coercive or compulsive quality to the sexual activity is more likely to indicate a child's own involvement. Experienced staff who constantly observe young children in play, may be particularly accurate in identifying play which is outside the norm of sexual activity, and in recognising knowledge which is unusual in its extent.

Masturbation. It is usually the quantity and uninhibited nature of a child's masturbation which arouses an adult's concern. Such excessive masturbation is likely to be a sign of underlying emotional problems of which sexual abuse, its associated feelings and relationships may be a cause. More specifically, a child who has been sexually aroused through repeated abuse may repeat the experiences compulsively, sometimes using hard objects. It is, however, unlikely that excessive masturbation could be regarded as diagnostic of sexual abuse.

Sexualised relationships. This refers to some children's way of relating to men, where a sexualised verbal or physical quality is noted. Young children may refer to a man as a boyfriend and suggest sexual contact. Others may touch the man's genitalia, invite or activate masturbation. In older children, such relating may amount to explicit promiscuity and arouse serious suspicion of previous sexual abuse. The sexual 'abuse' of younger children by adolescents is also likely to be based on previous sexual abuse of the older child.

Child psychiatric problems and learning difficulties. As indicated in Table 4.1 and previously discussed, the abusive contact itself and consequent guilt, or the relationships within the family, may all lead to emotional or behavioural disturbance. In childhood, the latter may manifest itself in many non-specific ways, which encompass much of child psychiatric practice. Low self-esteem in older girls may be the only sign of a well-recognised pattern in later life.

Learning difficulties may be one consequence, arising from the child's preoccupation with other aspects of her life, occasioned by, and in association with, the abuse.

Family life and relationship patterns. There is a growing awareness of certain relationship patterns which are more likely to be associated with child sexual abuse. A distant relationship between a mother and daughter, at times amounting to emotional or physical absence of the mother, is one such pattern. Another facet of this may be a child who holds a parental role in the family, particularly when in apparent parental partnership with a man. This latter relationship may assume an exclusive quality. Less specificity can be ascribed to the parental relationship which may be openly acrimonious, or sexually or covertly conflictual.

Some families appear to maintain vary loose intergenerational boundaries and appear underorganised, one aspect of which may be chaotic sleeping arrangements. Multiple child sexual abuse may be one correlate of cross-generational confusions.

Non-accidental injury and child neglect may be accompanied by sexual abuse. Abused parents are more likely to have abused children, and siblings of sexually abused children are at risk.

Alcohol abuse is often associated with child sexual abuse and may lead to the abuser's apparent or actual amnesia for the abuse.

Proceeding from suspicion to disclosure

When suspicion arises from outside the family, both direct and contextual information should be sought; the more non-specific the alerting signals, the more circumspect the enquiry must be.

A central difficulty for outsiders who suspect that a child has been sexually abused is awareness of the need to convey these suspicions to social services and to the police who would normally expect to approach the family immediately.

The dilemma is that premature communication of suspicions to the family may be counter-productive. When the family of a child who has not yet talked is approached by Social Services, the police, teacher or doctor in an unplanned way, the family may silence the child or refuse access to her. Such a direct enquiry may well constitute a warning for the secret of the sexual abuse to be guarded more closely, for fear of the consequences of discovery. It may also prejudice a future working relationship with social workers. In this respect, much greater caution is required than would be normal professional practice, in which the counsel is for openness and sharing of concerns with those giving rise to it.

Ultimately, only strongly suggestive physical signs and the child's word will constitute definite indicators of abuse. Whilst physical signs (like a fracture on an X-ray in cases of non-accidental injury) cannot be erased, the child's word may well be lost and must therefore be carefully preserved.

Using a Place of Safety Order to remove a child who is suspected of being in danger but who has not reached the emotional readiness to disclose, or who is as yet unaware of the abusive nature of the sexual contact, may be perceived as a violation of the child. Unprepared families who initially seek medical advice (but in which sexual abuse *may* be occurring), feel particularly enraged and betrayed if suspicions are pursued interprofessionally without their knowledge, especially if abuse is subsequently not proven. For these reasons it is important that careful planning always precedes active investigation of suspicion, which should not involve removal of the child, unless it is believed that, due to the traumatic nature of the abuse, the child will only be able to disclose after she is removed from the family. Investigation may begin with interprofessional enquiries which in turn may bring to light previously ignored symptoms, signs, information about previous sexual offences and even unrecognised partial disclosures. Many of these concerns do not apply if a mother openly presents her suspicions to a professional.

The various ways of proceeding, according to the nature of the suspicion, usually include preliminary interprofessional consultation:

1. Table 4.1 indicated symptoms (sy, *) of which the child would be aware and which are suggestive of abuse. The professional to whom such symptoms are presented is in a position to enquire of the child directly how the symptom could have occurred. The enquirer, preferably someone known to the child, will have to assess the degree to which the child feels free to tell, based particularly on the closeness of the child and her mother to the possible abuser(s). Leading or suggestive questions should at this stage be avoided with young children. Older children, who are likely to be aware of the existence of child sexual abuse, could be asked about the possibility of having been touched in a sexual way. Indeed, a very direct enquiry is appropriate to all children who run away from home, or who harm themselves. Hesitation by the child, who might be seen on her own, could be cautiously explored, enquiring about possible fears of the consequences of talking. No pressure should be put on the child at this stage. A proportion of children will partially disclose the abuse at this time, particularly when a symptom of the abuse is the reason for the contact between the child and the enquirer. Other, possibly convincing reasons for the symptom may be discovered, leading to removal of the suspicion, or suspicion may remain unresolved.

2. Physical signs (si, *) which are suggestive of sexual abuse are generally discovered in the context of an examination in which a suspicion of sexual abuse has already arisen. The child can then be told of the finding and the enquiry can proceed as outlined above, under (1).

3. The situation is somewhat different if suspicion arises due to the child's suggestive behaviour. Sexualised play and 'premature' awareness may well be noted in a nursery or infants' school setting, or occasionally during psychotherapy with a child. Older boys who engage young children in sexual activity should be suspected of having themselves been abused. The adult, who has observed and knows the child, could calmly explore with her or him the source of the sexual knowledge, but without suggesting the possibility of the child having been abused. Questions such as 'where have you seen this?' and 'who else does this?' might well lead to a partial disclosure. The same approach, by a familiar and trusted person, could also apply to children who are observed to

sexualise relationships, or who avoid men. Children who indicate their possession of secrets might be helped to divulge them by exploring the need for the secret and their fear of the consequences of breaking it.

4. An initial medical examination of a very young or pre-verbal child may also be indicated and may lead to findings which are highly suggestive of abuse. These would then justify an approach to the family and a request to talk with the child, possibly using anatomically correct dolls.

5. Suspicions of sexual abuse may also arise during professional contact with the family, for instance in family therapy or in the course of social or probation work. The nature and source of the suspicion will require clarification, and consultation with colleagues is important. Disclosure in a group such as a family meeting should not be pursued since it is very unlikely to come forth.

6. Alternative causes of other, less specific signs and symptoms should also be explored, in the awareness that child sexual abuse may coexist with other difficulties.

The common thread advocated here is a direct approach to the child by a person known to the child, with or without the mother, enquiring in an open-ended way about the possible source of the suspicion, or the feared consequences of talking. This may be regarded as tricking the child into betrayal, but the enquirer would be supported by the high degree of suspicion of abuse. This approach is very much more likely to enable the child to begin disclosing the abuse than a formal disclosure interview, however expert or skilled the interviewer.

The degree to which suspicion remains is a matter for professional judgement and should next be discussed in a planning meeting involving a specially designated and trained social worker and police officer, and other relevant professionals. The purpose of this meeting is to share information on the basis of which to determine the least detrimental and most appropriate nature and timing of further investigative and child protective steps (these are discussed in Chapter 5). Unlike in a case conference, it may be decided not to inform the family immediately. Only exceptionally would statutory child protective steps be invoked on the basis of unsubstantiated suspicion.

Partial disclosure – the child speaks

Reasons and timing

When a child tells someone, inside or outside the family, about aversive sexual contact with an adult, it can be assumed that she would like the secrecy surrounding that contact to be broken. It can also be assumed that, at least in part and at that instant, she would like the abuse to cease. This form of *intentional* disclosure is made more often by older children. The reasons for disclosure may be directly related to the current status of the abuse: for example, emotional and physical discomfort, fear of the increasing likelihood of full intercourse, or increasing threats and pressure. In this context, a particular precipitant to disclosure occurs when an abused adolescent girl embarks on a heterosexual peer relationship. The response of the abuser to this developmentally appropriate, although sometimes promiscuous, departure may be to attempt to restrict the girl's activity, perhaps violently. More rarely, disclosure occurs as an act of vengeance against the abuser. A child may also decide to disclose her abuse at a time when she fears abuse of a younger sibling or another child.

Although clearly not fortuitous, the reasons for disclosure at that particular moment are not always immediately apparent. A talk dealing with sex education, particularly if child sexual abuse is mentioned, may be a precipitant. This is happening increasingly with the recent advent of explicit training in self-protection now being offered to children. Disclosure thus precipitated may relate to current or past abuse, the latter continuing to constitute a burden of guilt and confusion carried by the child. It is the preoccupation with this incomprehension, and varying degrees of guilt, which often lead to disclosure. Under these circumstances, talking about what has happened may be an attempt to make sense of the experience and gain relief, but without a clearly articulated intention of stopping the abuse.

A more recent phenomenon, related to the more open manner in which child sexual abuse is being treated, has been the disclosure of previous abuse by a child who has been placed in an alternative home. These children have waited for safety before being able to talk of their experiences.

Younger children may mention sexual experiences to a friend, teacher or parent, without intending to bring about cessation of the abuse through this revelation. Such a possibly casual disclosure is less likely to be a conscious cry for help, being motivated more by a need to air an experience that is perceived by the child as disturbing, unusual, confusing or possibly frightening. This is termed here an *unintentional* disclosure.

Who discloses to whom?

The majority of children wish to tell their mother about the abuse. Many do so, some repeatedly. The likelihood of, and circumstances leading to, a child telling her mother vary and are dependent upon several factors. The younger the child, the more likely the first disclosure is to be to the mother. Younger children have greater difficulty in comprehending the abusive experience, and the mother is usually the person to whom a young child turns with physical soreness, and emotional or cognitive discomfort or unease. Younger children are less likely to be fully aware of the negative consequences of disclosure and may disobey instructions by the abuser not to tell, impelled by their own developmentally appropriate inability to contain their anxiety. The more distant the relationship between the child's care-giver and the abuser, the more likely the child is to disclose to her mother. Conversely, if the abuser is, for example, a grandfather or current step-father, or uncle of a child being cared for by her grandmother, it is more difficult for the child to disclose to her care-giver than when the abuser is the estranged father or a family friend.

In response to disclosure, the mother may become alarmed and distressed for her child and she may immediately feel very angry towards the abuser. She may previously have harboured suspicions, paricularly if abused herself, possibly by the same abuser. The confirmation of her suspicions might lead to relief and enable her to pursue the protection of her child. When there is a continuing relationship between the mother and the abuser, the mother's natural first move will be to approach the abuser, who is likely to deny the allegation strenuously. This may lead the mother to gain awareness of her pre-existing and now exceedingly uncomfortable position between the abuser and her child. The confusion and turmoil engendered in the mother by disclosure, particularly when faced by denial from the abuser, may lead the mother to disbelieve the child. Many children later talk about the times they have disclosed and not been heard. However, uncertainty or overwhelming concern for her child often leads the mother to seek help.

Some mothers, themselves suspecting abuse of their child, pursue their suspicions by questioning the child or the abuser. If the suspicions are confirmed, outside help may then be sought. In other cases mothers who have themselves been sexually abused may well be particularly sensitive to clues, which they may nevertheless wish to suppress from their own consciousness. Fear of the assumed consequences of disclosure, which are often based on their own experiences, become obstacles to stopping their child's abuse. Indeed, this is one of the factors which leads to child sexual abuse becoming the chronic experience so often encountered. Many other mothers, however, seek direct help.

What of those children who do not disclose to their mothers? These include older girls who are aware of the consequences of disclosure, often feeling protective of their families in the face of the predicted disruption to family life that disclosure will bring. In addition, sexually abusive relationships which carry a degree of enjoyment for the girl, often when the abuser is not a member of the immediate family, are less likely to be disclosed to mothers. There may be a wish for the relationship to continue, particularly if needs unmet within the family are being, albeit maladaptively, fulfilled. The associated guilt further deters the girl from disclosing. Again, those factors which lead to non-disclosure are concurrently maintaining the abuse.

A grandmother, aunt or sister are sometimes regarded as trustworthy confidantes. Their response is dependent on their relative commitment to the whole family or the alleged abuser and to the child's predicament. This relationship determines whether this form of disclosure will breach the secret or maintain it.

Siblings who witness abuse meet with the same range of responses when talking about their observations. Some are burdened by helpless guilt, carried silently for many years.

The role of the outsider receiving a disclosure

Outside the family, the child may tell a teacher, a friend who is known to have a close relationship with her own mother, or more rarely a social worker or indeed the police. The disclosure at this stage is usually only partial, and it is likely that the abuse will be found to be of longer duration and greater extent than initially suggested.

The role of the adult receiving the disclosure is initially to listen uncritically. Beyond gaining an understanding of the nature of the abuse, pressing for more details is not necessarily helpful at this point, since a full elaboration interview will have to be conducted. At this time, an acceptance of what is being said, conveying that the story is being believed and that the child is not in any way blamed for her involvement, is of the greatest help. The child should always be reassured that, despite inevitable misgivings, disclosure is the best course for her to have taken.

At this stage, children or their mothers may frequently request that the disclosure is kept in confidence and not divulged to anyone else. It is not possible to honour this request, and hope for it must always be sympathetically but firmly dispelled. It is always important to hear the discloser's reasons for wanting confidentiality, as her anxiety will only be allayed and trust in adults maintained if her misgivings and fears are heard and acknowledged. This may avoid a subsequent retraction of the account. It is generally possible to give an undertaking that no further action will be taken before first explaining it to the child, and a promise to keep her fully informed should be made.

The issue of confidentiality often arises again at later stages. The desire for confidentiality is instinctively felt by some professionals and embodied in codes of practice, particularly in the medical profession. It is therefore important to be clear about the reasons for diverging from one's normal practice, reasons which are now widely accepted in dealing with other forms of child abuse. Confidentiality will not protect the child from further abuse, nor will it lead to resolution of those distorted relationships that have enabled the abuse to occur. In the area of child sexual abuse, there is a real danger that confidentiality in the professional world will merely mirror the secrecy reigning within the abusive family or relationship, the former thus becoming paralysed by forces within the latter.

While the role of the first receiver is primarily to listen and comfort, it is useful to obtain some limited and specific information, where appropriate and possible. For the puposes of possibly obtaining forensic evidence, and for police investigations, it is important to establish the last time the abuse occurred. This question should be posed incidentally, the reasons not necessarily being presented at that moment. It is preferable to outline further plans to the child when these have been formulated by the various disciplines concerned, rather than to raise the child's anxiety by mention of these highly emotionally charged consequences. Information about the timing of the most recent abuse is also important in assessing the degree of risk to the child at the time of disclosure. It is important to note, however, that as well as understating the degree and frequency of the abuse at initial disclosure, the girl may, for emotional reasons, also describe current abuse as occurring only in the past. It is also helpful to know to whom in the family, or outside, the child has spoken and who is likely to believe and support her. These questions are less likely to be appropriately asked of young children.

Since the act of disclosure is likely to precipitate a crisis in the child's and the family's life, the child's safety must be secured by ensuring that, until further plans are made, she remains in the environment in which she felt safe enough to divulge the information.

Social workers are often consulted by those first receiving a disclosure; it is therefore necessary to consider in some detail these specific situations.

Disclosure to a teacher

Teachers are not infrequently the recipients of intentional disclosures, especially by older girls. Having responded as outlined above, teachers should inform the head teacher. Social Services are then notified via the education welfare service, who should be alerted by the head teacher.

Understandably, a school may wish to contact the parents directly, in the service of maintaining a good and trusting working relationship with the family of the child. What has to be considered here is the attendant risk of the child being silenced by the family before she can make a full disclosure and receive protection. The more credible the child's account appears, the closer the abuser is to the child's care-giver; and the more difficult it has been for the child to confide in her mother, the more appropriate it will be to notify Social Services. Subsequent approaches to the family can be made by Social Services, with or without a member of the school staff or the police. If this latter course is decided upon, it is important that the reasons for it are accepted by the school and conveyed to the child. Otherwise, a situation may be created very early in the complex process of intervention in which one very important agency, the school, is alienated. This can lead to later interprofessional conflict and misunderstanding, which ultimately adversely affect the child.

Disclosure to a doctor

Children are more likely to be taken to the doctor by their mother, be it a general practitioner, a community paediatrician at school or a clinic, or a doctor in a hospital accident and emergency department. The doctor may find him- or herself in a difficult position. Particular issues arise here in relation to confidentiality, conflicting loyalties, professional autonomy, and the need for and timing of a medical examination. The first issue has already been considered. A general practitioner who is possibly also the alleged abuser's doctor, may see himself facing conflicting loyalties to the child and the abuser. This difficult position requires resolution, since the abuser's need for help is as evident to the doctor as are the child's needs for protection. Consultation with colleagues and a sharing of the responsibilities are likely to be helpful and necessary. The question of professional autonomy is a familiar one in cases of other forms of child abuse, in which the principle of interprofessional co-operation has been accepted as being the best course to pursue in the interests of the child. The need to inform Social Services therefore applies equally in cases of child sexual abuse.

The question of the medical examination is a most vexed one, since this is the specific task of a doctor. As will be discussed in detail later, the timing and nature of examination, and the professional designation of the most suitably qualified doctor, are complex issues. Suffice it to say here that ideally an examination should follow a full disclosure, and that the child should only be examined once. A doctor, confronted with an initial, partial disclosure, is not usually in a position to adhere to either of these recommendations, since what is expected of him or her is to inspect the child and pronounce diagnostically. In that situation, a brief history and a brief examination of the child, including an *inspection* of the genital area, is an appropriate compromise, which may need to be followed by an expert examination. If there are acute symptoms or signs, a fuller expert examination, including the forensic aspects, should be pursued.

It is useful to find out the mother's concerns and explanations for the child's condition. Equally importantly, the doctor should enquire directly from the child how she was hurt. It is important to enquire in an open and non-leading manner, without pursuing a detailed account. On the basis of his or her findings, the doctor can then proceed with informing Social Services, with the knowledge and agreement of the mother, and of the child if she is old enough to understand.

If the mother withholds consent for notification, the doctor will have to continue to explore the mother's reservations and possibly encourage her to report herself. Consultation with another professional experienced in the field of child sexual abuse may be of help.

Disclosure to the police

Unless criminal investigations of an immediate nature appear appropriate, as in cases of notification immediately following a single assault by a stranger, the response to the child and family should at the outset involve notification to and co-operation with Social Services. This should certainly precede a medical examination, unless the child has been injured and is in need of medical treatment, or there is a clear likelihood of forensic evidence being available.

Disclosure in the course of therapy

As in other settings, such as school, the disclosure must find its way to Social Services. The question of whether to inform the mother first, deserves careful consideration.

A particularly difficult dilemma arises when sexual abuse is revealed in the course of psychotherapeutic work, either with a family or with an individual. Questions arise both in relation to confidentiality, which is necessary for the psychotherapeutic relationship to be maintained, and in relation to technique, which may well have been reflective and interpretive, rather than investigative. Pursuing the abuse might jeopardise the therapy, yet there is a need to protect the child. If it is believed that abuse is continuing, it is unlikely that disclosure by itself will lead to cessation of the abuse. The therapist is faced with the difficult task of abandoning the therapeutic role, hopefully temporarily, in order to pursue the prevention of further abuse. Much of psychotherapy is concerned with fantasy and conjecture, and the therapist now finds her- or himself being faced with, or having to respond to, a secret which calls for acknowledgement rather than interpretation. Here, experiences are not being unconsciously re-enacted in transference, but consciously named, possibly for the first time. The child may be testing the safety of an outsider's response. The therapist's response may be crucial in determining whether the secret will be reburied or allowed to be aired. The most difficult task is convincing the child or the family about the need for breaking confidentiality, and it may be an advantage to request a colleague's involvement. Since it is very likely that the period of abuse is of some duration, time will be well spent in exploring the likely and understandable resistance by the child or family to pursuing protection. An assurance can be given that the therapist will not proceed without fully informing the patient or family, and the family could be encouraged to report themselves to Social Services. There is a distinct danger that without social work involvement, the prevailing forces surrounding the child will prevail and overpower the therapist's individual endeavours to contend with the sexual abuse within the therapy.

The process initiated by the disclosures in all these settings rests on the assumption that children who begin to talk about sexually abusive experiences are very likely to be telling the truth. There is currently no evidence to suggest that, apart from the very rare occurrence of a psychotic illness, young children relate explicit personal sexual experiences which are based on fantasy rather than reality. Very occasionally, older children may make false allegations as a means of retaliation against a person by whom the child feels wronged. A parent who is involved in an unresolved, usually marital, dispute may occasionally allege, or falsely induce a child to allege, sexual abuse, as a means of furthering the dispute. These children are unlikely to make spontaneous allegations, and the information gathered about the family is likely to alert the professionals to the possibility. A professional decision will then need to be made about the advisability of a formal interview with the child. While the conclusion may be that sexual abuse has not, in fact, occurred, it is nevertheless likely that a child and family in this situation are severely troubled and in need of help.

Common pathways

Ultimately, the great majority of initial disclosures find their way to Social Services. In accordance with child abuse procedures, Social Services should inform the youth and community section of the police. Joint planning and investigation by the police and Social Services now commences with a preliminary search of their respective files, which may yield pertinent information already known about the child, family or abuser. The extent of further enquiries will depend on the degree of urgency perceived by the designated social worker and police officer at this stage. If time permits, information about the child and the family may be sought from general practitioners, health visitors and the education welfare service. The relative urgency and time available for further enquiries are determined by the child's immediate physical and emotional safety and the likelihood of the child retracting the disclosure or being silenced.

From this starting point, information is sought which will further the building up of a contextual picture surrounding the abuse. This particularly includes knowledge about relationships within the child's family and immediate network. It is at this stage that social workers and other professionals have the most demands made upon them.

Retraction

A partial disclosure may be rapidly followed by a retraction. Providing the allegation of child sexual abuse is not false (which it very rarely is) the disclosure must be seen as a way of enabling the child to gain some relief from the burden of the abuse and the secret. If in the process of initial disclosure the child is believed, then the comfort afforded by this experience may have the effect of enabling her to gain sufficient emotional strength to retract the allegation, thus preserving the status quo and avoiding the feared full consequences of disclosure. Equally, a half-hearted investigation by the professional network, remaining inconclusive and without a clear plan or future involvement with the child and her family may serve to enhance the continuation of the abuse. The abusive relationship or family are now reinforced by the withdrawal of visible concern by professionals, which may well be construed by the family as society's expression of trust and confidence in the family and the abuser. This process is akin to opening a window fleetingly to allow entry of sufficient light and air to ensure continuation of life in a dark and stuffy room. It is a process encountered not infrequently in sexually abusive relationships or families (Summit, 1983). Partial disclosure which is not followed up may thus enable the abuse to continue for longer, some of the immediate stress having been relieved.

Against this possible risk must be weighed the equally grave consequences of active intervention in a relationship or family in which abuse is later found not to have occurred, despite suspicions. This is the nature of the dilemma facing the professional network, particularly social workers.

While retraction may halt the legitimisation of statutory or police involvement, a continuing dialogue between the child and family and an outside agency is indicated. A retraction does not explain the reason for the preceding disclosure. A child who makes false allegations must be regarded as very troubled and in need of therapeutic help, which is likely to include an exploration of her family relationships. Further counselling, casework or therapy with a child who has retracted her previous allegation may, on the other hand, enable the true picture of abuse to emerge subsequently. Alternatively, this work may facilitate changes in family and other relationships, such that the abuse will cease.

5

The Process of Validation and Decision-making

In this chapter we consider the validation process, during and following which decisions will be made about the likelihood of abuse having occurred and about the identity of the abuser. This process also leads to an evaluation of requirements for child protection, the appropriateness of legal proceedings in civil or criminal courts, and therapeutic needs, based on the principle of the best interests of the child. As described in Chapter 4, the process of validation of suspicion or elaboration of a partial disclosure is a complex one, requiring the gathering of information from child, family and other sources. This requires careful planning and co-ordination, as well as some anticipation of the appropriate professional responses to the possible outcomes of the investigation.

The interview

Unlike other forms of child abuse, sexual abuse frequently leaves no marks. Thus, although the medical examination may yield important information, the child's account of what has happened is of particular significance. Usually, this means that a definitive interview will be required.

The purposes of the interview

From the child's point of view, a definitive interview may provide one of the first opportunities to talk to adults who are ready to listen uncritically and calmly. This may afford great relief, particularly if the child is ready and able to describe experiences of which she may feel quite ashamed, and which she may have thought unmentionable. Reassurance given to the child that she is not responsible for the sexual activity in which she has been involved can be a central and positive factor, rendering the interview a therapeutic experience.

At the same time, the interview is designed to enable the child to tell as much as possible about the identity of the abuser or abusers, details of the nature of the abuse, the locations and circumstances in which the abuse took place, and its timing and frequency. Although often not applicable, the question of the truthfulness of the child's account nevertheless must be borne in mind, and indications of possible false allegations should be considered. The description of the abuse will also inform the subsequent medical examination. These investigative aspects of the interview are important partly for criminal proceedings against the abuser, since the substance of positive findings in the interview will form the allegation and 'statement' on the basis of which the police can then proceed to question the abuser, a process which may enable the abuser to take responsibility for the abuse. More immediately, the contents of an interview will form an important part of the body of information necessary to obtain protection for the child. The potentially very drastic nature of these protective steps lays a considerable burden of importance on the process and contents of the interview, and the more these are legally acceptable, the more likely the interview will be useful for the child's later welfare.

Both the investigatory and therapeutic aspects of the interview are primarily designed to learn about *what* happened to the child rather than *whether* the child has been abused. This latter step is more appropriately established in the process of pursuing suspicion and the facilitation of the first, partial disclosure.

Persons involved

The child. The only persons who have detailed knowledge of the abuse are the child and the abuser. The secret nature of this particular relationship ensures that usually there are no witnesses who can corroborate the abuse. At this early stage, it is unlikely that a true account of the abuse is obtainable from the abuser. It is thus the child, even if very young, who is the only available informant. Very few children have been found to make false allegations. There is an increasing body of evidence pointing to the reliability of even young children as witnesses. By virtue of being children, they possess less knowledge (in this instance sexual awareness) with which to falsify accounts. As far as children's memory and recall are concerned, several interesting facts have emerged. Children have been shown to be able to recall accurately events which occurred before spoken language was acquired (Jones and Krugman, 1986). Children do not forget more easily than adults do, but their recall is limited to their understanding of the events, so that the quantity or detail evoked is not a function of the maturity of the memory process but rather related to the familiarity and meaning of the experiences which are later remembered. The memory of both adults and children is better when applied to personally significant rather than to peripheral events. However, what is perceived a significant to a child may not be so to an adult and vice versa (Jones and McQuiston, 1985).

Interviewers – social workers, police and child mental health professionals. Child sexual abuse is a crime committed against a child. Social service departments have primary responsibility for the protection of the child, but it is the police who are in the best position to deal with the criminal aspect. This dual responsibility for responding to the problem calls for close co-operation between these two agencies. Both require evidence of abuse, albeit to different standards of proof. The criminal law which is designed to lead to prosecution and under which the police operate, seeks evidence which is 'beyond reasonable doubt'. The standard of proof required for child protection is based on a 'balance of probabilities'.

The police have a clear interest in interviewing the child at an early stage, in order to obtain an allegation which will permit them to interview the alleged abuser. Equally, since it falls upon Social Services, or their delegated agency, to ensure the child's protection from further abuse and her subsequent emotional well-being, it is clearly necessary for a social worker to become acquainted, at an early stage, with details of the abuse. In order to minimise further trauma by repeatedly questioning the child, it is most helpful for specially designated and trained representatives from both these agencies to be present at the interview of the child; the police officer should always be plain-clothed. As will become clearer, the agenda of such an interview is complex and, particularly where younger children are concerned, considerable skill is required. Currently other professionals, such as child psychiatrists, psychologists or psychiatric social workers often conduct the interview. This interim measure will be necessary until sufficient police and field social workers have been specially trained for this task, although very young, emotionally disturbed or heavily silenced children will continue to require more specialist interviewing.

There has recently been some debate about whether men should carry out interviews. The vast majority of abusers are male. Since an interview may well conjure up and reconstruct very detailed recollections of the abuse, it is suggested that the interview will be less likely to be perceived as abusive to the child if the interviewing pair includes a woman. (These considerations, regarding the gender of the interviewer, do not apply to later therapeutic work, since alternative models of trustworthy men are considered very important.)

Presence at the interview is not synonymous with active participation, which is best assigned to one interviewer, with the other observing and consulting.

The trusted person. It is highly desirable and almost always possible to have the child supported by a trusted person who is known to the child and who the child is confident will believe her story uncritically. This will usually be the person to whom the child has disclosed initially. Indeed, the presence of this link person between the child and the interviewers is most important in facilitating the process of the interview. The mother may or may not, therefore, be the appropriate person to accompany the child during the interview. Interestingly, mothers frequently volunteer that their child will talk more freely in their absence than in their presence. Sometimes, children may be given the choice.

Consent

The question of consent for the interview reaches beyond the law to the spheres of good practice, optimal conditions for the interview and particularly awareness of the likely need for later therapeutic work with the family. Legally, for social workers and doctors it is likely that if interviewing the child at that time and place can be proven to be 'in the best interests of the child', later litigation will not be successful. Strictly, however, a Place of Safety Order, for instance, does not in itself confer permission to interview or examine the child. The police, furthermore, require consent from a parent before interviewing a child.

This question of consent is more fruitfully reframed as a need for co-operation with the family, highlighting at this early stage the complexity of the relationships surrounding child sexual abuse. A parent is unlikely to raise objections to a full interview of the child by Social Services and police in cases of stranger abuse, that is, where there is no current relationship of any sort between the care giving parent and the abuser. These cases are, however, in the minority. In those more usual situations in which the abuser is known to the child and the parent, the presence of social workers or police may well constitute an obstacle, the former for fear of subsequent care proceedings, the latter because of the threat of court appearances and imprisonment. It is, nevertheless, not possible to offer full reassurance on either count. Co-operation can only be gained when the parent's misgivings or fears have been heard, and the procedures explained as being in the child's best interest.

The exercising of social workers' legal right to interview a child without parental consent is extremely likely to prejudice adversely later work with a family, whose very objections constitute pointers to the need for such work. Where difficulties in obtaining consent are predictable, and particularly with younger children, time and safe space may well be gained by admitting the child to a paediatric or child psychiatric ward, as is frequent practice in cases of other forms of child abuse. This may facilitate further dialogues with the family to allow investigation to proceed.

Although it is the parent who is in a legal position to give consent, an interview with an unwilling child or young person is unlikely to prove fruitful and may indeed constitute further abuse. Preparation of the child, in a manner appropriate to their age, is therefore important, but must not include anything (for example, suggested responses) which could prejudice the credibility of what will be said later.

The question of divulging the police presence to the child must be addressed. This will depend on the age of the child. It is suggested that knowledge of this fact would place an additional and unreasonable burden on a young child, who would not be in a position to comprehend fully the need for the police. With older children, withholding the information would constitute a breach of trust. This is especially so for those children who declare their fears of the consequences of disclosure in relation to the imprisonment of the abuser. To find themselves unknowingly incriminating the abuser would be unacceptable and compound their guilt. Older children therefore need to be told clearly who the persons present at the interview are, and the role they are fulfilling should be explained. Under these circumstances, it is likely that the older child will feel more comfortable without the use of a one-way screen. If the interview is to be video recorded, the reasons for this must also be explained. Understandable anxieties regarding confidentiality and the further fate of the recorded interview must be addressed.

A helpful distinction can be made between video recording the interview as an adjunct to note-taking, and later decisions about who, other than the interviewers, should be permitted to view the tape.

In the interest of a continuing working relationship with the family, consent should always be obtained from the child's current carer before allowing tape recordings to be viewed. An older child alone cannot give legally valid consent, but it is nevertheless important for the child to know who has heard and seen her account.

Setting and preparation for interview and timing

The interview should ideally take place in a quiet, comfortable room, devoid of interruptions, preferably with video facilities and possibly a one-way screen. Interviews should not be held in police stations, since in the context of child sexual abuse this setting is very likely to be associated with guilt, which is often already present in the child's mind.

As well as the child, a trusted person and possibly the mother, a social worker, a police officer and an interviewer, such as a psychiatric social worker or child psychiatrist, may all be involved. The presence of this number of persons, all gathered in one room, is unlikely to constitute an atmosphere conducive to a child's disclosure of intimate experiences. With younger children, it is possible for some of the people enumerated to observe the interview from behind a one-way screen, without the child's knowledge. Consultation can then still take place between the various persons involved. The interview of an older child is less likely to require a specialist interviewer, and the mother will either be present in the room, or wait elsewhere.

The child's full disclosure constitutes the starting point for therapeutic intervention, and must therefore be heard unimpeded and unsilenced, raising the question of optimal timing. Child sexual abuse has usually been a continuing experience for a considerable time before disclosure and, unlike non-accidental injury, does not usually constitute a life-threatening event. Consultation and preparation are more likely to serve the long-term interest of the child and family than instant and unplanned intervention. Included in this consultative and preparatory stage of interprofessional involvement is the gathering of information about the family. The family may be known to Social Services or the police may have some knowledge of the possible abuser. The greater the likelihood that the child may be intercurrently silenced by the family because the initial breach of the secret is perceived by them not to be in the interest of the abuser or the family, the stronger will be the need for careful interprofessional planning before informing the mother of further steps. Disclosure often precipitates a crisis, which is better dealt with if anticipated. The degree of urgency rises with the more elective and deliberate initial disclosure by a child. Equally, an account suggesting very recent abuse, particularly within the previous day or two, indicates the possibility of collecting material for forensic evidence, so rarely obtainable in most cases of child sexual abuse.

In cases where the concern about abuse has not been initiated by the mother, she should be informed before the child is interviewed and examined. This contact may be timed to occur while the child is safely in nursery or at school. Some aspects of the family relationships can be learnt about in this initial meeting with the mother. There is a need to gain an understanding of the quality of the relationships between the care-giver/mother and the alleged abuser, between the child and the abuser, and the child and the mother. The position of other siblings is also of importance. It is during this period of crisis that difficulties in relationships, which might otherwise remain hidden, come to the fore. Some children are clearly supported and safe in their caring environment, and here the degree of urgency for immediate validation and protection is less.

Indeed, the purpose of further investigation may be related more to protection of other children and society's wish for prosecution than to this child's needs.

The practice of placing such considerable significance and attention on a single interview rather than learning about the child's experiences more gradually over time, has raised questions for professionals, particularly those working therapeutically with children. While a more gradual approach might often be advantageous, the need for protection of the child including protection against pressure to retract her account, may well not allow for this. It is nevertheless important to achieve a reasonable balance between, on the one hand, the need to obtain an account from the child and, on the other hand, the degree of pressure applied in facilitating this.

The medical examination should normally follow the disclosure interview, unless physical injury is known to have occurred.

Video recordings

Video recording of the interview is of considerable value. It forms an undisputed record, and since interviews with younger children often involve the use of dolls, play and other non-verbal communication, it is preferable to audio recording. This record of the fuller disclosure has been found to be extremely valuable in helping parents and abuser to believe the child's account and acknowledge responsibility respectively.

The recent advent of video recordings of interviews has for the first time enabled the legal profession to observe part of the validation process by which clinical and social work decisions are made. In court proceedings, which not infrequently follow disclosure of child sexual abuse, the precise nature of the allegation and disclosure are frequently of considerable interest to the parties involved, as well as to the bench. While this development is to be welcomed in principle, it is important to ensure that the many non-verbal and contextual responses of the child that are not captured accurately on a video tape are not omitted in the evaluation of the interview. Furthermore, an assessment of the abuse cannot be based solely on one interview, which is only a part of a carefully planned information-gathering process.

The use of video recordings in criminal proceedings against the abuser, both at committal proceedings and full trial, are currently being explored. In the case of the former, this may make an otherwise unlikely prosecution more likely. In the latter, the use of video recordings may in future obviate the need for the child to give evidence against the abuser in court, if the rules allowing for a defendant to cross-examine his prosecution witness were to be relaxed in cases involving children.

Aids to the interview: anatomically correct rag dolls, drawings and play materials

As well as being a source of detailed and reliable information about the abuse, the interview is designed to afford some comfort. A room free of interruptions and distractions offers distinct advantages, while a low table, comfortable chairs, drawing materials, a few toys such as a doll's house and some cars, and anatomically correct dolls may all aid in making disclosure easier, especially with younger children. The dolls are available in various ethnic identities and include parents, grandparents, adolescents and children of both sexes. It is important to regard the dolls as useful aids for a child's communication with a trained person rather than as a diagnostic tool in their own right.

Children's names for parts of the body, particularly genitalia, are often very private, idiosyncratic or ambiguous. For example a child may refer to all genitalia, male and female, as 'willy'. The word 'bottom' is often used collectively, for all that lies between the legs. By inviting the child to draw, or point to, the precise part on the appropriate doll, a comfortable and at the same time precise mode of communication is established. The dolls, in particular, also offer a means of conveying to the child that the interviewing adults will not be shocked by explicit anatomy. The child can assign her own special names to the anatomical areas of the doll and demonstrate, rather than say, what has been experienced. The doll-persons involved in the abuse can be picked out by the child. This enables the child to participate actively in the interview, instead of being a passive recipient of the many questions which will necessarily be asked.

An initial period of free play with the dolls also allows for observation of the child's spontaneous play. There does not seem to be one pattern of play diagnostic of sexual abuse. Some non-abused children are very wary of undressing the dolls, even with explicit permission and encouragement; other children stop at the dolls' pants. An abused child is more likely to treat the adult male doll particularly roughly. She may readily and uninhibitedly undress the dolls and spontaneously enact explicit sexual activity between the dolls, or may insert fingers into the vaginal or anal openings. Sexually explicit play with the dolls is highly suggestive of a learnt experience, whether based on observation of sexual activity or actual involvement. Non-abused children do not appear to enact adult sexual activity when playing with these dolls. However, the fact that a child plays with the dolls freely and non-sexually, in a manner similar to non-abused children, cannot be claimed as evidence that the child has not been abused (Glaser and Collins, 1987).

Some children, particularly older ones, may decline the offer of playing with the dolls and may prefer to illustrate their account with drawings. For instance, a shy girl who hastily covered her drawing of a little girl by drawing a pullover over the body when asked where the 'belly-button' was, agreed to draw an undressed girl on another piece of paper, knowing that she could cover her nakedness with the clothed drawing. A child may also use drawings to illustrate their house or draw family members.

The process of the interview

It is difficult to conceive of a uniform format or sequence for an interview, since these depend on the age of the child, the state of willingness and readiness of the child to talk, and the degree of guilt which the child carries, both about involvement in the abuse and about disclosure and its feared consequences. Furthermore, there is likely to be a difference between the process of an interview the purpose of which is to help the child elaborate on experiences already partially disclosed, and one which is designed to establish whether abuse has occurred and to facilitate the first disclosure. Nevertheless, it is important for the interviewers to be aware of the areas to be covered in the interview and to relate these to the child's psychological position at the time of the interview. Few children anticipate the opportunity to talk openly and fully with eagerness and freedom from conflict. Younger children may only be very partially aware of the agenda of the interview. Several central factors determine the ease with which the child will talk. One is the nature and intensity of the non-sexual aspects of the relationship between the child and the abuser. Another is the nature and intensity of the relationship between the child's mother, care-givers or family and the abuser. The more involved and positive are those relationships, the greater is the conflict for the child. A further determining factor is the nature and intensity of the injunction to secrecy which has been imposed on the child. A notion that the child invariably perceives the interview as a long-awaited rescue mission may stand in the way of a sensitive, facilitating approach to the child.

The interview

INTRODUCTION	Using language appropriate to the child's maturity, it is important to begin by both helping the child to make sense of the interview and allowing her to introduce herself and describe her family and current context. Maintaining this balance is a delicate task, since few children would unquestioningly accept enquiries about themselves in a strange setting without wondering about their purpose. The aim is to guide the child towards areas of interest to the interviewer (without direct suggestion) whilst enabling her to tell her story.
CHILD'S KNOWLEDGE ABOUT PURPOSE OF INTERVIEW	It is helpful to enquire how much the child knows about the purpose of the meeting. Older children are usually very aware of this, younger children vary. Many children do not volunteer their awareness of the agenda.
FREE PLAY AND NAMES FOR ANATOMICAL PARTS	The child may choose to draw or play with the dolls freely, and this should be observed. If the child has not done so, permission to undress the dolls may later be given and this can be followed by establishing the child's names for parts of

the body. She may use the dolls to represent sexual activity and can be asked where she has seen this, who the dolls involved in the play are, or who else does this with whom. This may then lead directly into a description of the abuse.

ORIENTING THE INTERVIEW

Alternatively, the interviewer may guide the child towards talking about the areas which led to suspicion of the abuse or arose as consequence of it (without mentioning the actual abuse). These may include vulval soreness or bleeding, current admission to hospital, cessation of access visits to the (allegedly abusing) father, or the presence of the trusted person to whom the child has begun disclosing. This approach allows the child to link an account of the abuse with an experience to which she can initially relate more comfortably. With younger children, the dolls may then be incorporated into the tale. For example, the child, having identified the dolls as (named or unnamed) boy, girl, man or 'daddy' and woman or 'mummy', can then be invited to show where the girl doll has been sore and how she came to be sore, who is living at home or what sort of games the girl plays with the man doll. If appropriate, having reminded the child that she has already told the trusted person something special or private or that she has previously described a way in which she has played, the child can then be invited to 'pretend that the dolls are' those persons involved. It is preferable to allow the child herself to name the dolls as the persons in her life. Ethnically appropriate dolls are available, and where there may be doubt about the identity of the abuser, a suitable array of dolls should be provided from which the child may choose. Where the age is appropriate, a child's account can be followed by the request to 'show me the dolls', or use drawings. No doubts need then arise about which anatomical parts the child is referring to, and the child's own names for anatomical parts can be established.

In the absence of links being available or if the child is not amenable to engaging in this exploration, it is possible to approach sexual abuse more directly. An exploration of different kinds of physical contact between people is a helpful starting point. The word 'touch' may be thought by a younger child to indicate manual touch, and it is important that the child understands the wider meaning of the word. 'Good' and 'bad' touch are adults' notions and should not be assumed to be shared by children. Children are more likely to relate to bodily contact described as feeling different, 'funny' or uncomfortable. It is also possible to tell about other children who have spoken to the interviewer about having been touched by a grown up in a private or special part of their body, such as is covered by a swimsuit. The interviewer could then go on to ask if this child has had any such experiences, without suggesting the person of the likely abuser.

As the interview progresses, the child is thus encouraged to describe the sexual activities in which she has been involved, using as much spontaneous description, language and detail as possible. Interviews with older children are often easier to conduct, since there can be greater certainty about the consensual reliability of the language used. Even some older children, finding the interview stressful, may perceive the use of the dolls or drawings as a relief.

FULL DESCRIPTION OF ABUSE

The child may be asked to show whether she was standing up, sitting or lying down and the alleged abuser's position in relation to her.

WHERE ABUSE TOOK PLACE

In obtaining a full acount of the abuse, it is important to enable the child to describe where, geographically, the abuse took place, including in whose house and in which room. This is more difficult with younger children. It is often helpful to clarify this by suggesting that the child pretend that the table in the interview room is, for instance, the bed, that a box may be used for a door, or the floor for 'downstairs'. Drawings of the house are also helpful. The whereabouts, during the abuse, of other family members can then be clearly established. It is important to enquire which other doll, or person, may have witnessed the sexual activity, or who else was involved. Having established that the child was made sore by another person, a child may, for instance, be asked 'which of my dolls made the little girl doll sore?'. Equally important is the question of other abusers, and the younger child could be invited to say whether any other doll or person touched her in that way. Timing and frequency of the abuse are also important to establish, although younger children's concepts of time and

WHEREABOUTS OF OTHER FAMILY MEMBERS

WHO WITNESSED ABUSE, WHO ELSE INVOLVED

IDENTITY OF ABUSER(S)

TIMING AND FREQUENCY

frequency may well not be sufficiently reliable; there is then little value in pressing for these details.

SEEKING DETAILS OF FURTHER ABUSE

Abused children often find difficulty in giving a full account of all the abusive activities. For example, oral sexual contact such as fellatio tends not to be described spontaneously, and a child who may be able to describe mutual masturbation may not mention attempted intercourse, particularly an anal approach. The question then arises of how to enable the child to talk about the full range of sexual abuse, without suggestion. Questions such as 'did other parts of Daddy doll's body touch the little girl's fanny?' are preferable. The interviewer could indicate the range of anatomical parts, including more and less likely ones (feet, mouth, chest and penis, arm, etc.) from among which the child could choose. Alternatives such as 'did he use his hand or also his "willy"?' are more suggestive but still retain an element of choice for the child. Ultimately, it is important to establish or exclude all forms of sexual activity. Apart from the evidential criminal-legal importance of full information, it is very likely that a child who is able to tell only part of her story will be left feeling roused and burdened.

The elicitation of details about the state of sexual arousal of the man, such as whether he experienced penile erection, are more important from an evidential perspective than for the child's emotional well-being. The child could be asked to describe the penis, which way it was pointing ('show me on the doll'), and how it felt. If doubt about the abuse remains, a choice can be offered between 'soft' and 'hard'. Ejaculation is experienced as aversive by the vast majority of children, particularly if associated with oral sexual contact. Enquiring about whether anything 'came out' of the penis, what colour it was, where it went, its taste (if oral sex is described) and how it was removed are uncomfortable details, certainly for the interviewer and probably for the child. It is a matter for professional judgement at the time of the interview to decide whether the relief gained from the opportunity of talking and evidential requirements outweigh emotional discomfort for the child.

CHILD'S FEELINGS ABOUT SEXUAL CONTACTS

These considerations lead to the very important area of the child's feelings surrounding the abuse. Whilst the adults are likely to feel indignation on behalf of the child and very possibly anger at the abuser, the child's feelings may differ. Some children derive physical enjoyment from some or all of the abuse. Others have clearly undergone wholly traumatic and aversive experiences. It is therefore important to explore the child's feelings and experiences through open questions such as 'what did it feel like?' Clearly, physical pain and discomfort should be named. If the interviewer senses that the child derived some enjoyment, it is as well to say to the child, 'some children like being touched like that, and others do not. I wonder what it was like for you?' This is preferable to immediately terming the touch as 'bad', since that is likely to leave

SECRETS

CHILD'S
FEELINGS
TOWARDS
ABUSER

DEFINITION
OF ADULT'S
FULL
RESPONSIBILITY

the child feeling confused and guilty. Aside from the sexually arousing quality of the abuse, there are other important emotional aspects which require exploration, enabling the child to feel truly heard and understood. The majority of abused children are told not to talk about the abuse. This may or may not be accompanied by threats, including those of physical punishment, reception into care, imprisonment for the abuser, or divorce of the parents. Thus, even if some may not dislike all the experiences, nearly all abused children are aware of the forbidden or 'rude' nature of the activity in which they were involved. Further confusing to the child are the ambivalent, loyal or positive emotions which many children hold in relation to the abuser. Some are terrified of the abuser and others feel only hate. The latter are in the minority. If an interviewer dismisses the abuser as bad, this will only leave the child more guilty and confused. Rather, it is preferable to explore, even if only briefly, the nature of the relationship between the child and the abuser, and the quality of the almost invariable injunctions to secrecy. One might, for instance, enquire about what the abuser would say if he knew that the child was telling, and how the child knew about his likely reaction. The use of the word 'secret' is better initiated by the child.

Only then can one move on to define the adult firmly as wholly responsible, assuring the child that she is in no way naughty, bad, rude or responsible, either for the abuse or for disclosing it. Acknowledging one's awareness of the conflict and fear which the child may well be experiencing is more helpful than adopting a moralistic stance.

DEALING
WITH
RELUCTANCE,
ANXIETIES AND
FEARS

Resistance
The account so far assumes that the child is willing to talk. The closer the relationship between the child's care-giver and the abuser, or the child to the abuser, the harder the emotional task for the child. In this it is preferable to digress from pursuing the account of the abuse and return to it later, rather than persisting relentlessly. Reluctance to disclose can also be helped by exploring the anxieties which fuel this reluctance. One might say 'sometimes children want to tell someone about what happened to them, but they are worried about what will happen if they do. Can you understand why?' One may then go on to explore the reasons, and in the absence of the child volunteering any, it is possible to offer choices, including consequences to the child such as punishment or withdrawal of love. Some children are more fearful of their mother's reaction. Others fear the consequences for the abuser. Sometimes it is possible to enquire who would suffer most as a result of the disclosure and what form that suffering might take. The explicit naming of anxieties is more likely to help the child to talk. However tempting it might be to reassure a child that their fears are unfounded, this cannot usually be given with any basis of certainty and would further gravely undermine the child's already frail sense of trust. Some abusers do receive custodial sentences. Some mothers do

blame and reject their children, who may be received into care. Many fathers do deny the abuse, thereby calling their children liars. What can be given is a firm assurance that despite the child's misgivings, disclosure is nevertheless the best course of action. Experience has shown that the majority of children do appear visibly relieved at the end of disclosure interviews. Ultimately, however, a child's resistance must be respected, particularly when it becomes increasingly clear that from the child's point of view all is to be lost and very little gained from further disclosure. An initial partial disclosure may have afforded sufficient relief, and then be retracted. If the abuse nevertheless appears likely, then what can be conveyed is that the initial disclosure is fully believed, and symbolically held in trust by the adults who heard it.

Completion

CHECKING ACCOUNT WITH CHILD

At the conclusion of the interview it is useful to summarise the disclosed experiences briefly, checking for the child's agreement and the consistency of the account. If the descriptions referred to the dolls, it is important now to name the child and the adult clearly in place of the dolls.

The responsibility must again be laid firmly at the feet of the abuser, and the child praised for her courage and clarity. Next, the child must be helped to tell her care-giver or mother briefly about the abuse, if the latter was not visibly present during the interview (for instance, if she was behind a one-way screen). It is a heavy burden for the child to carry home

TELLING THE MOTHER

alone, and she must know that she will be supported by the adult to whose immediate care she returns. Mothers are often very upset to hear the child's full account, and time may have to be spent in allowing the mother to recover sufficiently to hear the account again briefly in the presence of the child.

PREPARATION FOR MEDICAL EXAMINATION

Finally, the way is paved for the medical examination to follow. The timing will depend upon how recently the child was abused. If the last contact took place within two or three days of the interview, examination should always follow on. A longer time interval since the abuse allows for postponement of the medical examination if this is felt to be appropriate for the child.

Most children and their mothers will accept the examination, to make sure that the child has not been hurt. Many children, particularly adolescent girls, harbour a great deal of anxiety and fear about the physical consquences of the abuse. A sensitive examination may go some way towards reassuring them. The interview informs the medical examination, and guides the examining doctor in what is required for the particular child.

EVALUATION

The assessment of the interview is based both on its content and process. The child's consistent and spontaneous accounts are of the greatest significance. The degree of knowledge which a child demonstrates should be related to the familiarity with sexual details which a child of this age would normally possess.

Also of importance are the body language and non-verbal communications observed. These include pauses and hesitations, diversion from and avoidance of certain areas, distress at certain points, lowering or averting of gaze, frozenness, sadness and relief. Their timing in relation to the content form an integral part of the evaluation of the child's experiences.

Mention must also be made about the indications of possibly false accounts by children. A child might be suspected of having been put up to making false allegations if she enters the interview ready to give a detailed account freely and unhesitatingly, especially when this is given with the consistent use of inappropriately adult phrases. This is most likely to occur in the context of an unresolved conflict between the care-giver and the abuser.

Repeated interviewing

In the event of a child's being unable to give an account of abuse, a similar second interview is unlikely to yield more information, unless there is a clear indication of a change in the child's circumstances, such as a greater sense of safety or permission to talk. Repeated interviewing would otherwise constitute further abuse of the child, or may lead the child to provide expected rather than valid information.

For the purposes of later prosecution, a signed statement is required. Young children are clearly unable to provide this, and an accurate transcription of the interview, signed by the observer or interviewer, is sufficient. Older children are usually required to make a statement themselves. This may be limited to signing a handwritten account of the interview, or entail a repeated description of the actual abuse, which may at times become protracted and exhausting for the child.

In the absence of video recordings it is often requested that the person(s) involved in interviewing the child meet with the abuser in order to provide him with a full account of the child's disclosure. This may also later be necessary if there is a change of care-giver for the child. If court proceedings, civil or criminal, ensue, the interviewer is also likely to be required to give evidence. It is therefore important that careful notes of the interview are kept.

The medical examination of sexually abused children

This is a very sensitive area of investigation, both for the child and for some professionals who, following specific experiences, regard the medical examination as a further potential assault on the child. Others, particularly the police, lay great store by the medical findings and are keen to proceed with this part of the investigation immediately.

The fact is that fewer than half the children who have been sexually abused have any findings at the time of medical examination. This is partially due to the nature of the sexual contact, and partially related to the fact that more long-standing sexual abuse, particularly when the abuser is very familiar to the child, rarely declares itself within a sufficiently short time of the abuse to allow for medical findings to remain.

There are many factors to be considered in relation to the examination. As regards the timing, this, as already mentioned, should follow the interview (which is equivalent to a medical history), except for very young children. In addition, there is the question of identifying *suitably qualified doctors*, the *location* of the examination and its *content*. These will all vary to some extent, depending on the type of abuse. Child sexual abuse spans a continuum ranging from an isolated incident of stranger assault to long-standing intrafamilial abuse. As Table 5.1 illustrates, the situations at both extremes appear as different entities determining very different circumstances and attributes of the medical examination.

The doctor

Social workers or police may well need to identify a doctor whom they will consider suitable to carry out the examination. Several

Table 5.1 *Attributes of medical examination*

In stranger rape/assault	Medical factors	In intrafamilial abuse
immediate or shortly post abuse	TIMING	variable, rarely immediate
probably indicated	COLLECTION OF SPECIMEN	less likely to be relevant
usually police surgeon	DOCTOR	variable, including GPs, paediatricians, police surgeon, community child health or family planning doctor
usually police station or surgery	LOCATION	variable, including GP surgery, casualty or out-patients, community clinic. Regrettably sometimes police station
	Child factors	
frightened but willing to disclose unless acutely shocked		frightened, worried, may not be willing to disclose
supported by mother		may not be supported by mother
feels wronged and recognises herself as a victim		may feel guilty and responsible

skills are required when examining a sexually abused child. The doctor will often find him- or herself faced with talking to young children and their anxious mothers or having to consider the particular feelings of adolescents. The examination should include a general paediatric and only exceptionally a full gynaecological one. Familiarity with the normal anatomy of young children and the appearances of the genitalia and anal region of abused children is a prerequisite, which currently are unfamiliar areas for many doctors. Forensic and microbiological specimens may have to be collected, the doctor must be available to carry out the examination at any time, and be willing, available and of sufficient seniority to give evidence in court.

For doctors to fulfil these criteria, further training will be required. They may be recruited from the ranks of police surgeons, hospital and community paediatricians, family planning doctors and general practitioners. The police are often responsible for arranging the medical examination, the results of which they may require before interviewing the alleged abuser. It is therefore very important to have locally available, specially trained doctors, whose services can be called upon whenever required by a social worker and the police.

Older girls certainly prefer a female doctor, and factors similar to those discussed when considering the gender of the interviewers suggest preference for female doctors wherever possible.

Location

There is no reason for carrying out medical examinations in police stations, which may well carry the implication of guilt for the child. If the examination is to follow the interview immediately, the two should be carried out in the same location. The child is usually accompanied by her mother or care-giver. Although the police may wish to be closely available, whether to transport any specimens collected or to obtain a statement about the findings, it is not usually necessary for a policewoman to be present at the actual examination. A social worker may appropriately accompany the child.

Consent

Under the age of 16, a parent's consent is required. Older children's consent should additionally be obtained.

The aims and nature of the examination

There are three broad aims to the examination:
1. medical;
2. medico-legal;
3. psychological.
The medical nature of the examination is concerned with determin-

ing the presence of actual injury, infection or pregnancy and recommending appropriate treatment. The medico-legal aspects are concerned with establishing the actual nature of the abuse, who the abuser was and whether force was used. The psychological contribution of the medical examination lies in the possibility of offering reassurance in the absence of findings or treatment for positive findings. The doctor who is able to indicate her belief in the child's account regardless of the presence or absence of findings is joining the supportive network surrounding the child.

It is accepted as part of normal medical practice that a history is taken before an examination is carried out. Indeed, examinations are always informed by the history if one is available. As part of establishing a relationship with the child to be examined, a doctor will usually ask the child about the reasons for the examination. One suggested way of obviating repeated questioning of the child is for the interviewing social worker to elaborate on the child's brief reply, in the child's presence. This continuity is often perceived by the child as very supportive. The doctor will then be in a position to decide on the nature of the examination. Usually, a general examination is carried out first, which is both reassuring to the child and necessary in looking for other forms of child abuse, such as bruising, scratching and lacerations, particularly in the genital area. Careful inspection of the genitalia includes looking for redness, swelling, bruising, lacerations and the state of the hymen in girls, and the penis in boys. There is a certain variation in normal and intact hymenal shape and size, and familiarity is gained through experience. Careful anal inspection must also be included. Recent full reports (for example, Hobbs & Wynne, 1986) indicate the frequent presence of anal signs in both boys and young girls. It is important to note that anal signs return to normal after a period free from abuse. Digital vaginal or anal examination should only be carried out with specific indications. Forensic specimens from the genitalia or mouth are only likely to be sought within a short time of abuse, when the child's clothes, particularly pants, should be preserved unwashed. If the child has complained of vaginal discharge, a careful search for infection should be made and swabs taken.

Where there is a suggestion of the possibility of sexually transmitted disease, a visit to a special clinic should be arranged, optimally timed for one week after the abuse. In older girls, pregnancy testing may be considered appropriate. The social worker may need to accompany the child and pursue these later investigations.

The examination may be brief or more prolonged and varies according to the needs of the child. Children rarely require sedation if the examination is carried out calmly and unhurriedly. The child's response to the examination, particularly of the genitalia, may provide an indication of the emotional effect of the abuse. Some children will strenuously resist examination, indicating the degree of traumatisation. Others will accede too readily, assuming sexualised postures and indicating the degree of habituation which regular abuse has caused them.

It is always important for the doctor to ensure that the child's and mother's concern have been acknowledged, and that both are told of the full findings of the examination at its completion. The offer of a further consultation, either with the examining doctor or appropriately appointed other, is often appreciated. This is particularly important for adolescent girls, who very frequently harbour anxieties about the potential damage which the abuse may have caused them.

A common misconception arises on the frequent occasions when the medical examination yields no abnormalities. These negative findings may be interpreted by a doubting mother as proof of the fact that no abuse has taken place. Some mothers feel reassured by the fact that their daughter has remained a virgin, assuming that all is now well. Children often assume that they are thereby disbelieved. The police may on occasion not pursue matters for lack of medical proof. It is, in this context, helpful to note that oral sex leaves no marks, and that vaginal penetration is defined as entering beyond the labia minore which may leave no permanent mark, rather than actual penetration of the vagina. However, as medical expertise and experience of this work increases, it is likely that the medical examination and its findings will assume greater importance in the process of investigation.

From the doctor's point of view, careful recording of all findings including the child's response is important, since medical evidence may be required later. The doctor's evidence should not be expected to prove the occurrence of abuse, but may be stated as being compatible with abuse, or establishing it beyond reasonable doubt.

Post-disclosure decisions

On the basis of the nature of the suspicions, family relationships and social circumstances, evaluation of the interview with the child and findings of the medical examination, a number of decisions will have to be made, some immediately and some at the case conference later. The importance and urgency which some decisions now assume stand in contrast to the acceptability of a possible delay during the pre-disclosure phase. That delay may have entailed the risk of exposing the child to further abuse in the intervening preparatory stages. This risk may well have been accepted in the interest of ensuring a co-ordinated and planned professional response at the time of crisis. Why the post-disclosure urgency? The contrast lies in the staggered timing of the crisis in the professional and family systems respectively. Partial disclosure leads to a crisis for professionals. There the anxiety is firmly contained until full disclosure and possibly medical findings emerge, comprising not only a declaration outside the family, but also exposure of the secret within, precipitating a crisis for the family. At that time, from the child's vantage point, absence of a clear, immediate response which includes being believed and protected will be perceived as a betrayal of newly burgeoning trust and may well lead to devastating disillusionment.

A preliminary view will have been formed by the investigating professional team, which includes social workers, police and doctor, about the likelihood of abuse having occurred. If this is likely, two decisions, preceding the case conference, may be required. One concerns the immediate placement of the child and siblings, the other the need to question the alleged abuser.

At this point, the child is more likely to be in danger of further emotional and physical trauma from disbelief, pressure to retract and punishment for disclosure, than from immediate further sexual abuse. In order to safeguard the child accordingly, different requirements arise in relation to abuser and care-giver. Immediate protection from the abuser can only be ensured if all contact between the child (and possibly siblings) and the abuser is supervised by an adult who is not part of the existing family–abuser system. The practical implications of this statement are that if the child and the abuser have been living together, then one of the two must leave.

The social worker carries the difficult task of helping the mother to overcome or contain her reactions (which may include shock, disbelief, anger and possibly guilt) to help her accept the need for a possible choice between child and abuser; and to encourage her to maintain a benevolent and supportive attitude towards the child. Tangible evidence of this benevolence would be the mother's declared belief that the child was abused and is not to blame for the abuse, for the disclosure and for the possible consequent departure of the abuser. It may be appropriate to allow the mother a short period of time in which to collect herself and reach a decision. Some children and their siblings are, however, removed on a Place of Safety Order, particularly if there is reason to suspect that the mother or care-giver has played any active part in allowing the abuse to occur, or if it is likely that the child will in some way be punished for the disclosure. Whilst this move may be necessary for the child's immediate protection, it is likely that without careful and age-appropriate explanation by the social worker, it will be perceived by the child as further punishment and therefore proof of her guilt. It is also very helpful if the mother can explain to the child her own reasons for reaching this painful decision. Some older children choose not to return home at this stage. Some abusers agree, as an expression of their sense of responsibility, to leave home.

For those many children who do not live with the abuser, immediate decisions may not need to be made, so long as reliance can be placed on the child's parents to ensure that there will be no unsupervised contact with the abuser. If a child is in hospital, decisions may await the outcome of the case conference.

Of more immediate consequence is the fact that the contents of the disclosure interview constitute an allegation, permitting the police to question the alleged abuser. The more specific the information, including any additional medical findings, the more able the police are to obtain an admission or, in thereapeutic terms, a statement of responsibility from the abuser. Whether the police will proceed to interview the abuser and the child's mother or care-giver immediately or later, will depend on the perceived urgency to protect the child. The police have full discretion as to the worth-whileness of interviewing the abuser. This decision is largely based on the quality of the disclosure information, its specificity and consistency, and may also be influenced by later interdisciplinary case conference decisions. Whilst interviewing the abuser may well not yield a prosecution, the fact of being questioned by the police can have a profound and important impact on the abuser and indicate to the child and family the seriousness of the situation. On the other hand, the absence of subsequent prosecution may be wrongly interpreted by the family as a finding of 'not guilty'.

The obtaining of an initial statement of responsibility is pivotal in determining the course of later events for the child, the family and the abuser. An unconditional positive statement by the abuser now, not to be retracted later, is one of the most beneficial developments for the child's subsequent emotional welfare. The assumption of responsibility to the point of pleading guilty will also spare the child from the need to give evidence in the eventuality of a trial. It is clear that the methods employed by experienced police officers in obtaining an admission by the abuser are of considerable importance. An admission made but later claimed to have been forced and therefore retracted will be of little positive value and may indeed prove to hold further detrimental consequences for the child.

The police, as part of their interdisciplinary co-operation, recognise the therapeutic as well as the criminal-legal value of a positive statement of responsibility. Serious consideration is currently being given to the possibility (already active in some states of the USA) of showing the video-taped recording of the disclosure interview to the alleged abuser in an attempt to help the assumption of responsibility. Whether this is construed as the imposition of undue pressure is a matter for debate and decision in a legal and civil liberties context. The acceptance by the abuser of the video-taped recording as a true record of the child's statement may constitute partial agreement, and therefore corroboration, in legal terms. However, current sentencing policy, which often leads to imprisonment, necessarily dictates that a man will perceive the police investigation as tantamount to encouragement to gaol himself. Many sexual abusers do not possess such strengths.

The case conference

This follows the recognised child abuse procedure. As well as a pooling of knowledge about the child and family, specific information may be available from the police about the abuser's response to questioning, and from the social worker about the mother's and family's response to the disclosure of the abuse. The conference will further determine the likelihood of abuse having taken place and is in a position to make certain *recommendations*:

1. It may be decided to place the child's name, and possibly those of siblings' on the Child Abuse Register.
2. It may also recommend that an interim care order should follow a Place of Safety Order already obtained.
3. In complex cases or where there is uncertainty about whether criteria satisfying juvenile court proceedings will be met, a recommendation may be made to initiate Wardship proceedings. It is important to note that the question of whether abuse has occurred will again be examined in these court proceedings.
4. In cases of separation of children from their families, there will be a need for decisions about the nature of access, ensuring protection of the child from pressure to retract and from blame.
5. A fuller assessment of family relationships is likely to be sought which will help determine the longer-term safety and welfare of the child, siblings and whole family, as well as pointing to therapeutic needs. In the vast majority of cases, further involvement by a named social worker will be required.
6. The case conference will also be in a position to recommend a view regarding the desirability or otherwise of prosecution. This decision will then be passed to the Crown Prosecution Service, who will further determine the legal advisability of criminal proceedings, basing the decision largely on the availability of corroborating evidence.

It is thus apparent that final decisions about placements and therapy may have to await the outcome of different and unrelated court proceedings, during which the child and family wait uncomfortably in limbo. Whilst the initial crisis may now be past, the longer-term work of supporting the child, the family and possibly foster parents or residential workers begins. This task, which may also include further evaluations and assessment, is largely carried out by social workers, with consultation and specific involvement from more specialist teams or child mental health services.

Finally, in those unresolved situations where suspicion remains, supportive or therapeutic work with the family or the child, aimed at those related areas of concern which led to the initial suspicion, may ultimately lead to disclosure or help to avoid further abuse. The most important step here is the identification of a trusted person, often a social worker, for the child outside the family. It is then possible that, in the context of this relationship, the child will feel free to talk and unburden herself, although it is important that neither child nor worker perceive the primary aim of the relationship to be an investigatory one.

6

After Validation: Aims of Further Professional Involvement

This chapter is concerned with the identification of the needs of the abused child and family and the definition of intervention goals. These might be termed the 'what' and 'why' of the post-disclosure professional response. In Chapter 7, the 'how' – that is, specific therapeutic settings and techniques, including group work, individual and family work and their relative merits – will be considered in greater detail. Team and interprofessional issues will be addressed in Chapter 8.

The responsibility for assessment, identifying needs and ensuring their fulfilment lies with social workers. They are also likely to have a considerable involvement in the implementation of these tasks. As the process unfolds, the fulfilment of the post-abuse needs will require addressing some of the very issues which allowed the abuse to occur, as well as attempting to resolve feelings about the abuse itself and the inevitable consequences of disclosure.

Intervention is likely to involve different individuals, dyads, groups and the whole family at different times. It will vary with the age of the child, the duration of the abuse, and the time elapsed since the abuse occurred. In the post-abuse period, needs are heavily dependent upon the degree, nature and stage of legal involvement, including child protection and criminal proceedings.

The interventions considered here are based on a *thereapeutic* approach aimed at comforting, and making sense of bewilderment, confusion and anger; it is also concerned with protection for the child and with changes which may offer new experiences in relationships and an improvement in self-image for individuals.

110

There are several considerations which underpin the social worker's co-ordination of the post-disclosure thereapeutic task. These are indicated in Table 6.1.

Table 6.1 *Considerations underpinning post disclosure intervention*

1. **Needs of the child**
   — protection from further sexual abuse and inappropriate sexual relationships;
   — acceptance and belief of child's full account of, and feelings about the abuse;
   — freedom from blame or responsibility for the abuse, the disclosure or its consequences;
   — opportunities to explore child's own feelings about the abuse and its effects (emotional, social, physical and sexual);
   — belonging to, and integration in, a caring family, free of guilt;
   — help in restoring ability to form positive, trusting and developmentally appropriate relationships with caring adults and peers.

2. **The child's setting**
   — assessment of extent to which child's immediate family, social network and educational setting meet the child's needs;
   — therapeutic intervention to explore and resolve difficulties preventing child's needs being met;
   — consideration of placement in an alternative home if needs are not being met;
   — importance of concept of permanency planning;
   — dealing with issues arising in substitute placement, especially (a) child's feelings of separation and change independently of, and additional to, the abuse; (b) concerns of substitute parents over caring for sexually abused child, and the effects on the family.

3. **From crisis to therapy**
   — crisis intervention to explore family relationships, origin of difficulties and potential for change;
   — formulation of therapeutic goals to ensure meeting of child's needs;
   — exploration of feelings, relationships and circumstances: (a) pre-dating abuse, (b) related to abuse, (c) as consequence of disclosure.

4. **Professional issues**
   — co-ordination and (a) surveillance of fulfilment of child's needs with possible statutory component, (b) formal therapeutic task;
   — clear division of labour, with avoidance of interprofessional splitting and rivalry or confusion.

In the remainder of this chapter the many post-disclosure aspects are considered in relation to the child as an individual and as a dependent person in her social context, although the two are closely interlinked. It is neither possible nor appropriate to adhere to a rigid plan, but certain priorities for the child can be identified. The primary consideration is ensuring the child's safety from further abusive experiences.

Protection of the child's sexuality

Within the family

The seemingly simple first step of protecting the child constitutes, in practice, an extremely complex process which, if pursued comprehensively, will involve most of the issues underlying child sexual abuse. Whilst this process may in some cases prove to be relatively simple, this is often not the case.

The fact of disclosure will not by itself ensure cessation of the abuse, nor protect the child from further inappropriate sexualisation of relationships. Furthermore, many abusers who have been imprisoned as a recognition of their responsibility for the abuse, and who have not received appropriate therapy, return to abuse the same and other children.

In those situations where the abuser is previously known to the child, the abuse forms a constituent part of a network of pre-existing relationships. If meaningful change is to be achieved, the forces which govern these relationships are likely to dictate the need for therapeutic work beyond the declaration of the abuse.

As mentioned in Chapter 5, protection from re-abuse can only be ensured by limiting the contact between the child and the abuser to, at most, supervised situations, until the abuser has been able to take responsibility for the abuse and has responded to appropriate therapy.

In ensuring this initial separation between child and abuser, it is undoubtedly more appropriate for the abuser to depart than for the child to be removed. Only if this separation cannot be ensured is alternative care likely to be required. The risk of a devastating sense of disillusionment and a lack of trust is considerable if a child who has disclosed abuse is later re-abused in the same setting.

The protective role of the mother or non-abusive parent(s). Following disclosure of child sexual abuse, it is a critical social work task to assess the degree to which the child's care-giver can now offer her protection against further abuse. To a large extent, what will determine this will be the nature and closeness of the relationship between the abuser and the care-giver. For example, separation of abuser and child and effective protective action by the child's parents usually present relatively little difficulty if the abuser is a stranger to the family and sufficient grounds exist for the police to proceed against him. There are also situations in which disclosure can mobilise a care-giver's protective abilities by revealing abuse of which she or he was unaware. This may be the case when the abuser is a family friend or is in a relationship with the child that exists relatively independently of the family.

The difficulties of ensuring protection for a child multiply as the abuser's emotional proximity to the family increases. In particular, where there is a close relationship between the abuser and the care-giver, the care-giver is often faced with an extremely painful choice: break the relationship with the abuser or lose the child. Thus, a mother who undertakes to exclude her husband from the home will need considerable professional support to maintain this decision in the face of emotional and economic strains and losses, and perhaps threats of violence from the abuser or his family. The mother may also be blamed by others affected by her resolve, such as the abuser's children (in the case of step-child abuse) or his own extended family. The social work task is both to provide as much support and counselling to the mother as possible, and to monitor the success with which the mother keeps to her declared intentions.

The most difficult obstacles to protection are the care-giver's internal ones, which may well stand in the way of her or his resolve to protect the child. For example, in situations where the abuser is a grandparent, the parent may have to choose between loyalty to the grandparent or the safety of the child. In other instances, unexpressed anger at the child for precipitating a separation from the abuser may be linked in the mother's mind to a secretly harboured belief that the child has in some way seduced the abuser, possibly in competition with her. Some parents find the guilt which their child's abuse evokes in them an intolerable burden, leading to a negative view of the child who, in the absence of the abuser, may be perceived as the source of the parent's emotional discomfort. These feelings will be intensified by a pre-existing poor or distant mother–child relationship or the low self-esteem which mothers who were themselves abused may feel. Some of those parents who were themselves victims of sexual abuse find difficulty in maintaining an awareness of the reality and damage of their child's abuse, probably because of the absence of a therapeutic intervention in their own childhood. To do so would reawaken the pain of fully acknowledging the harm which their own abuse caused.

As part of a long-standing position in the family, some sexually abused children hold a parental role, often in relation to the parent(s) and to other siblings. Indeed, the sexual abuse may sometimes represent an expression of this role. Under these circumstances, mobilising the family's protective abilities may be a very difficult task, involving both the exploration of ambivalence and the alteration of ingrained patterns of family relationship. Social work assessment and therapeutic intervention merge into one another as the goals for change in such relationship patterns are explored and defined.

If the mother or other care-givers can be helped to fulfil the child's needs for protection, a cornerstone for the future adjustment of the child has been put in place, and can lead on to work which addresses the child's need to be believed and freed from blame and responsibility. The ability of the family to protect the child is thus a critical measure of the overall acceptability of the child's placement at home. If, even with social work support, it appears that the child is not adequately protected at home from sexual or emotional abuse, then alternative permanent care will have to be sought, through care or wardship proceedings. This decisive step is likely to precipitate considerable anger, pain, sadness and rejection in the child, but nevertheless allows for the open expression of these feelings, as well as for their resolution within the provision of alternative care. The most difficult situation for the child is a continuing relationship with a mother whose undecided or ambivalent attitude leads to unresolved confusion for the child and militates against any meaningful adjustment and resolution of feelings.

Protection from new sexual abuse

Sexual abuse which was linked to a meaningful relationship between child and adult, which was experienced as pleasurable by the child and which was long-standing, is very likely to render the child vulnerable to further abuse. Whether the child initiates new sexual contact as a learnt means of obtaining gratification, is unable to decline the 'offer', feels powerless to resist, or seeks warmth and care and receives a sexual response, varies from case to case. Younger children may still regard this sexual contact as a normal part of relating to adults. An aspect of the social work and therapeutic task with the children's care-givers, whether biological or substitute parents, is to help increase their awareness of this dangerous likelihood.

The child's contribution – self protection. One of the damaging effects of child sexual abuse is that many abused children learn to regard sexual contact as an integral part of relating and as a necessary component, or even the main ingredient, of the expression of affection and caring. Those sexually abused children who have suffered from emotional deprivation, for whom the sexually abusive relationship may have offered their only caring experience and who lack a sense of their own worth, are particularly vulnerable. In these circumstances it can be helpful to teach children ways of differentiating appropriate from inappropriate forms of touch and sexuality. This involves helping the child learn to value her own body and person, distinguish between good and inappropriate touch, and as a consequence be able to say 'no' to unwanted approaches. Another aspect of this self-protection is learning about the unacceptability of secrets and the identification of a person to whom the child can talk if approached. Older children will also require contraceptive advice. However, a child will only be able to exercise her newly acquired wisdom when she is able to benefit concurrently from good, caring, non-sexualised and non-blaming relationships, and after she has been helped to understand that she was not responsible for the abuse. One danger of assertiveness training programmes for children is that they may introduce the notion that sexual abuse is a result of a child's failed self-protection.

Protection from inappropriate sexual involvement with other children

As was discussed in Chapter 2, mutual sexual exploration between peers is a part of normal childhood. The degree of preoccupation with sexuality varies between children and its explicitness is dependent on the children's knowledge. Mutual inspection and touching is probably quite common, as is the use of sexual words such as 'fucking' without awareness of the full meaning, the word being synonymous in some children's minds with love or hugging. Children who have witnessed or been told about the act of intercourse may try to mimic it with their peers. Abused children are privy to greater knowledge and may well wish to involve their peers in the recreation of their experiences. They may thus attempt to have intercourse with other children, insert fingers into the vaginal and anal orifices, or initiate oral-genital contact. In the context of post-abuse protection, such sexual activity may be harmful to the abused child by dint of leading her to be rejected or disapproved of, or to being held responsible for involving others, particularly younger children, in a sexual relationship. Indeed, for younger children this sexual play with an older abused child may in turn merge into a sexually abusive experience. In addition, an increasingly recognised occurrence is the abuse of younger children by sexually abused adolescent boys. This area is of particular concern to nursery staff and teachers, as well as to foster and adoptive parents and residential staff responsible for the care of sexually abuse children.

The therapeutic task here is to limit the child's sexual activity without inducing further guilt, without curbing natural peer sexual exploration, while still enabling the child to retain a concept of sexuality as enjoyable and permissible, albeit in the appropriate context. Abused children need to be taught about socially acceptable touching and sexual activity, generational boundaries and ownership of one's treasured body. Since informed consent is not part of sexual abuse, the notion that consent must be sought from the other before embarking on sexual play must be taught to the abused child as a new concept. Therapeutic groups for sexually abused children may be the best setting for considering appropriate sexual play with other children (see Chapter 7).

The child's emotions

The nature and degree of emotional discomfort which abused children feel vary greatly, both among individuals and between groups of children who share abusive experiences. There are, for instance, differences between those children who were abused when young but whose abuse was terminated by early intervention, and those who continue to be abused over many years. Other differences arise in relation to the emotional proximity of the abuser to the child, the mother and the family, and especially to the degree of secrecy and coercion associated with the abuse. Secrecy is particularly harmful, but the effects of coercion are more complex: coercion will increase a child's fear and sense of helplessness, but sometimes reduces her sense of guilt.

Disclosure offers the prospect for change and implies a process of readjustment for a child who has had to learn to deal compliantly with coercion, confusion and guilt (Summit, 1983). Some indication of the new stress precipitated by open declaration and cessation of the abusive relationship is gained from new behavioural and emotional disturbance which some children show (Jones and McQuiston, 1985). Once the need for denial and acceptance, which enabled the child to survive emotionally, has been removed, the full force of the many repressed feelings is released. These feelings include guilt, sadness, confusion, anger, isolation, fear and anxiety. The sources of some of these are listed in Table 6.2.

It is likely that a child who makes an intentional disclosure or who makes a clear plea for help has at least begun the process of readjustment, whereas discovery of abuse following an outsider's suspicion may find a child emotionally unprepared for the change in her life.

In addition to the guilt and self-blame experienced by most sexually abuse children, there is a wide range of other emotions that may operate to leave them confused or disturbed. The intimate sexual feelings evoked by the abuse and the pleasure which some children derive from the sexual contact are often difficult for children to voice and for professionals to hear.

Ambivalent feelings of anger and fondness for the abuser are not easily expressed in a context which strongly disapproves of the abuser and the abuse. This is often a dilemma for boys, who may feel some positive identification with their abuser. Anger at the absence of protection or a protector may at first be voiced in private, as will the exploration of the guilt, detailed above. Fears for one's future sexual functioning and of damage to sexual organs are often harboured but infrequently mentioned without prompting, possibly making referral to a family planning doctor an appropriate

Table 6.2   *Some sources of guilt and self-blame*

Predating abuse

— Relationship difficulties in the family, especially marital (or equivalent) disharmony
— poor/distant mother–child relationship
— child abuse

Directly related to sexual abuse

— involvement in forbidden, secret sexual activity
— enjoyment of the sexual contact
— 'allowing' abuse to continue
— not talking about the abuse

Arising as consequence of disclosure

— act of disclosure – betraying of secret and abuser
— the fact of police involvement
— mother's anger/discomfort/loss
— sibling's anger/discomfort/loss
— prosecution process – testifying against abuser
— imprisonment of abuser
— reception into care*
— separation from abuser, e.g. stopping access*

* Both often perceived by child as confirming his or her guilt.

course of action. Many sexually abused children describe a sense of isolation, feeling that they alone carry a guilty stigma and believing that their abusive experiences are unique. This stigma may be particularly burdensome for boys because of the homosexual nature of their abuse. Children nearly always lack an acceptable account of their experiences, the absence of which often leads to social discomfort in the face of anticipated or actual questions from peers and others. Thus they may feel unable to explain separations within their families, moves of home and their evident upset which they may find difficult to hide. Therapeutic groups offer a good setting in which to explore their feelings and develop ways of mastering these very understandable anxieties; in addition, all children will require the opportunity to talk about their experiences with a trusted person, be it their mother, foster parent or social worker. Children who continue to be heavily burdened by guilt and self-blame are particularly likely to benefit from more intensive individual psychotherapy.

Young children whose abuse is disclosed early are often less guilt-laden and experience less anger than older children who have acquired greater awareness of the consequences of the abuse and in whom the emotional accommodation to the abusive relationship has been more long-standing. Younger children are more likely to feel confused by the sexual experience and the considerable upheaval which disrupts their life after discovery of the abuse. They may feel a sense of loss at their separation from, or cessation of access to, the abuser. They are likely to find difficulty in comprehending and accepting separation from a parent who is considered by professional agencies to be unable to protect the child from further abuse. This separation, often undertaken in order to preserve a life free from further abuse and prevent the consequences of long-term sexual abuse for a child who has not yet been profoundly damaged, requires careful explanation, since the child is unlikely to be aware at this early stage of the seriousness of her experiences. As these children grow up, their questions will develop with their maturity. The early circumstances and decisions therefore require careful documentation by the social worker, so that the child may later be given a full explanation for events which shaped her life before she was ready to comprehend them fully.

The acceptance of children's needs for a permanent family placement has led to a heavily increased burden on, and therefore wait for, court proceedings. Children may linger in short-term placements, awaiting the outcome of civil court hearings at which a final 'finding' (or not) of abuse and definition of their needs will be made. These civil hearings may sometimes await the outcome of a criminal trial. It may not be possible to offer therapy specifically addressing sexual abuse to a child thus waiting if a possibility exists that the child will be returned to a family who deny the abuse. Children in this situation (and their carers) require a great deal of support, explanation and acknowledgement of their overwhelming wish for permanency. Since the early interruption of sexual abuse is a new professional venture, it is not possible to predict with certainty the response and adaptation which children who have been preventively placed away from their homes will experience. Young children whose abuse is not physically traumatic and who are able to remain with their mother or parents will probably suffer less long-term psychological damage from the sexual abuse, providing that the family circumstances surrounding the abuse are sensitively handled.

A particular predicament: children who are required to testify in criminal proceedings

This eventuality potentially faces many abused children in the post-disclosure phase. In practice, however, the current law which dictates that an adult cannot be brought to trial on the uncorroborated evidence of a minor ensures that few children are required to testify. It is only in cases where some independent corroboration exists or where alleged abusers initially admit the abuse, but later claim duress and retract their confession, that the child's evidence is likely to be required. Only children of sufficient maturity are deemed eligible to testify. No particular age is attached to this concept, which is based on police and lawyers' assessment of the child's ability to distinguish truth from untruth. It is rarely considered below the age of nine years. Whilst this currently only involves a minority of children, the situation may change if more prosecutions are brought, the change being based on an increasing belief in children's accounts despite denial by the abuser. The question of which legal response is most likely to be in the child's interest is a difficult one, and probably varies from case to case. Children, and their care-givers, do undoubtedly benefit from the knowledge that the responsibility for the abuse is clearly shown to rest with the abuser. The difficulty arises in determining at what cost this relief should be gained. If imprisonment is the cost, then for some children the burden of guilt is heavy, especially if imprisonment results from the child's testimony in court. Other children feel fewer doubts about their wish and ability to testify against the abuser, recognising the process to be a just one. There is usually a delay of many months before the trial, and the abuser's plea of guilty or not guilty may remain uncertain throughout this period, leading to added tension and often barely tolerable anxiety.

Professional and care-givers' misgivings often rightly centre around the actual court proceedings. The child may be facing a feared (or loved) abuser for the first time since the abuse. The higher the court, the more intimidating the setting. The process is an adversarial one, and defence barristers are rarely trained in child psychology, whilst using their utmost skill to fulfil their assigned role of defending the accused. The criminal law reserves the right for the accused to cross-examine the prosecution witness, in this case the child, and cross-examination it often is, with the avowed intention of discrediting the evidence. Preparation of children for this experience is necessary, even if the child is unreservedly willing to be involved. The preparation, usually undertaken by the social worker, includes visits to a court in progress before the trial and actual practice in replying to possibly hostile or very searching questions. In exceptional circumstances, children's written evidence has been accepted.

In the foreseeable future it is unlikely that changes will come about in the English criminal law which will dispense with the right of a defendant to cross-examine his prosecution witness. Video recordings of the child's testimony are therefore unlikely to be admitted as evidence. However, procedural changes are now being put forward which would ease the ordeal for the child. Using live video transmission, these changes would permit the child's evidence to be observed in another room by the jury and the accused, whose responses must be observable by the jury. The setting for cross-examination could then be a comfortable room, in which the child would be questioned by the defence and prosecution counsel, preferably not clad in full legal regalia. The child could also be supported by a trusted and neutral person. These seemingly minor changes would considerably lessen the intimidating nature of the proceedings.

The child and the family

Children in their own families

Social workers and others involved with sexually abused children generally attempt to find ways of enabling a child's needs to be met within the natural family setting. It has already been stressed that the first criterion in assessing the viability of this aim is the extent to which the family is able to protect the child against further emotional or sexual abuse. This will increasingly become a long-term and difficult task in those many cases of early discovery of abuse in young children. However, even if protection can be assured, there may be a number of other emotional and relationship issues in the family which require solution. This will be particularly the case where there was a close relationship between the abuser and the child's family, particularly the mother, but in all circumstances there are likely to be difficulties in family functioning that a social worker will have to be concerned with. In what follows, we consider the key relationships separately in order to define potential goals for therapeutic intervention.

The mother–child relationship. The child's relationship with the non-abusing parent(s) is a critical one, within which there may be difficulties predating the abuse and which will be compounded if the abuse was intrafamilial and of long duration. This relationship may, for instance, have a distant or a conflictual quality which militated against disclosure and allowed the abuse to continue. The child may have previously tried unsuccessfully to tell her parent about the abuse, and anger about a perceived lack of protection may only gradually emerge after disclosure. The mother may harbour feelings of resentment against the child for attracting the abuser, or for 'causing' a separation from him which has physical, emotional or economic consequences for the whole family.

Social work and therapeutic intervention in these circumstances aims to help both parent and child to express their feelings, ensuring that the child is protected from excessive parental anger, while being enabled to recognise the mother's predicament. Resolution requires the parent's open acceptance of the child's feelings which may include some continuing fondness for the abuser. The parent's undefensive acknowledgement of their often inadvertent contribution to the child's emotional discomfort is part of the healing process and the re-establishment of appropriate intergenerational boundaries.

The abuser and the abuser–child relationship. There can be no certainty that abuse will not recur by an abuser who has not acknowledged the abuse, since in the absence of such an acknowledgement, there is no starting point from which change could commence. Unfortunately, however, only a minority of abusers confirm the child's allegations. This is due to a number of factors. The private and public shame, and particularly the real fear of imprisonment, stand in the way of admission of the abuse. Even among those who are able to acknowledge the sexual contact, a number deny the abusive nature of the sexualised relationship by maintaining that no harm was intended or sustained, or by claiming to have acceded to invitations, if not pressure, from the child. This situation is particularly common in the minority of cases where the abuser is female: the abuse may be regarded as an expression of closeness and affection, particularly as coercion is less likely to accompany this sexualised relationship. Many abusers have themselves been physically, emotionally or sexually abused or were reared in families in which sexual abuse occurred. They often lack the very autonomy and strength required to respond in the way which offers the greatest help to the child whom they have abused – namely, to take responsibility for the abuse.

There are techniques which social workers and others dealing with abusers can use to try to offset the impact of these factors which inhibit acceptance of responsibility. Where confrontation and persuasion fail, exploration of the consequences of hypothetical responsibility sometimes succeed. By enabling the (suspected) abuser to name the anxieties, which may include fear of suicide, that stand in the way of admission, it is sometimes possible to help him face the feared reality. It has also been found helpful to allow the alleged abuser to see the child's account of the abuse on video tape. Currently, this is permitted practice in some states of the USA. In this country the legal profession and the police are actively considering this possibility. Objections, which claim that this practice would impose unreasonable moral pressure in pursuit of an admission, are scarcely understandable. A contrary view which regards a viewing of the child's disclosure as satisfying the alleged abuser's rights, would appear more appropriate.

The social work task with abusers is made very complicated by the current legal situation which, if understandable from a criminological point of view, is extremely unhelpful to the child and her family. It may be, for instance, that custodial sentencing policies will have to change before a greater rate of assumption of responsibility by abusers will occur. It is likely that the prospect of a therapeutic outcome to criminal legal proceedings, such as a suspended sentence together with a probation order with the condition of treatment (and residence away from the child where appropriate), would encourage more abusers to admit to the abuse. Whilst imprisonment clearly expresses society's disapproval of abusers, its deterrent effect is less certain, since abused children are often told by the abuser that the consequence of breaching the secret will be to send him to prison. Furthermore, some abusers are not helped in the process of admission by current legal rulings in relation to evidence. Many abusers are aware or are correctly legally advised that an adult will not be prosecuted on the uncorroborated evidence of a minor. Corroboration of any kind is rarely obtained, including the most helpful one – that is, confirmation of the abuse by the abuser. The abuse is not usually observed by a person old enough to bear acceptable witness, physical examination rarely yields findings stronger than compatibility with the abuse, and forensic evidence is even rarer. Where an abuser and a child have lived together, even forensic evidence may be discounted by explanations such as non-sexual contacts between abuser and child within the household.

Despite the child's clear statement, the abuser may nevertheless perceive the situation as offering an opportunity to escape from punishment. So long as the child's uncorroborated account continues to be invariably regarded as insufficient evidence to merit a trial, the abuser's denial appears to be accepted, offering little incentive to the abuser to alleviate the child's sense of guilt or remove the label of being a liar. Much more work is required to change this situation so as to increase the likelihood that the abuser will assume responsibility for his actions and thus help the child after the abuse. It is only after such an acceptance of responsibility that work can begin with the abuser to reduce the likelihood of his further abuse of children.

Despite the abuse, children and abusers frequently seek to maintain or renew their relationship, particularly if this predated its sexualisation. The question of whether a relationship can be successfully and reliably desexualised is an open one. Observations and accounts would lead one to believe that without carefully planned expert therapeutic work with an abuser and child, the potential for re-abuse, which may continue beyond childhood, is considerable. The abuser's capacity to give his genuine blessing to the child's appropriate peer sexual relationships may be regarded as some indication of positive change. The child will need to be able to express her anger at the abuser and rightly expect the abuser openly to own full responsibility for the abuse. This will be of great significance to the child, regardless of the future constellation of the child's family. The abuser may be an estranged father, uncle, grandfather or older brother, none of whom would be expected to rejoin the family. The most painful constellation is where the adult who is the sole care-giver in the family then proceeds to sexually abuse one or several children. Despite the considerable attachment that would exist between the abuser and the children, it is unlikely that the children would ever be fully protected if returned to his care. Supervised access may offer the best prospect for maintaining a relationship.

An open question remains regarding the desirability of continued, albeit supervised, contact between a child and an abuser who does not take responsibility for the abuse. In this commonly encountered situation, the child is effectively being called a liar by the abuser, perpetuating the guilt or confusion which she may be feeling. On the other hand, she may harbour genuine loving feelings towards him, and want to retain some vestige of their previous relationship. The social work predicament here is to weigh up the emotional dangers and benefits to the child of continued contact between child and abuser, considerations that go beyond those of the child's physical safety.

Mother or non-abusing parent(s)—abuser relationship. Where the mother and the abuser had a relationship that was in any way meaningful, it is important that the future status of the relationship – whether it is to be continued or dissolved – should be formally established. This is necessary regardless of whether the abuser continues to have contact with the child, because the crisis of the disclosure and of professional intervention may produce numerous changes in the non-abusing parent as well as in the abuser. For instance, as the crisis of disclosure recedes, the mother's previous, perhaps intensely held, feelings for the abuser may re-emerge. On the other hand, a mother may become more autonomous and less dependent in relation to the abuser who may have been her father or cohabitee. A father may wish to attempt to escape the tyranny of the abusing paternal grandfather. The abuser's own deprivation may require recognition and sympathy, albeit not with the intention of absolving him from responsibility for the abuse. In the absence of resolution of these relationships, it is the child who may continue to suffer, as well as the adults and other family members, particularly siblings.

Siblings. The siblings in the family may have had little attention paid to their needs. They may still feel confused and in the dark, or know what happened without being able to admit their awareness publicly. There are occasions in which siblings, too, may have been abused, but awareness of the consequences of disclosure may cause them not to divulge their own experiences. In the not uncommon cases of stepfather–daughter sexual abuse, the siblings may experience the loss of their biological father, and blame the abused child for this loss. For preventative and protective reasons, non-abused siblings are sometimes placed in alternative families. This is a particularly difficult decision, the reasons for which require very careful explanation by the child's social worker and, if the child is too young to comprehend, meticulous documentation for the child's later information. Occasionally, siblings feel rejected for not having been selected for the abusive attention. Open discussion can allow siblings to describe their perceptions and enable them to acquire an understanding of the confusion around them.

Family issues. Many families will continue to live together without the abuser. Some families do express a strong wish to be reunited, even after the abuser may have served a custodial sentence. Every family member may wish for such an outcome. In these families, beyond issues of protection of the abused child and other members, it is likely that a careful therapeutic exploration of the abuser–mother relationship will be required. Families have a need to make sense of the upheaval and disruption which they have undergone. The advent of the sexual abuse may have offered an apparent solution to family problems, for instance diverting conflict from a marital or sexual dispute within an outwardly harmonious and intact family and this may now become revealed. Other conflicts and difficulties may lie unresolved in the wake of the crisis of discovering sexual abuse. Meaningful change would only come about following marital and family therapy, in which issues other than sexual abuse would also be considered. Alcoholism, physical illness, financial difficulties, parenting issues and difficulties with other children in the family are but a few examples. An undoubted prerequisite for the future survival or rehabilitation of a family is their ability to talk openly about the abuse and, where he is to be included, for the abuser freely to assume responsibility for it. If, despite efforts, resolution of the conflict between adults or the requisite establishment of intergenerational boundaries and adult responsibilities does not appear possible, the situation would move into the familiar social work arena of marital break-up and questions of access, with additional caution over any unsupervised access between the abuser and the child or children.

Substitute families

Children's perception of their position when coming into substitute families is frequently that the move constitutes the ultimate proof of their guilt or undesirability to their natural parents and is therefore a punishment and rejection. Sexually abused children, in particular, may harbour such feelings. Substitute parents, in turn, are likely to require and request specific guidance from social workers in anticipation of receiving sexually abused children. Concerns and anxieties often include the following:

1. Should the sexual abuse be mentioned by the substitute parents, and if so, in what context?
2. How should the parents respond if the child introduces the subject?
3. What should other children in the family be told?
4. Is the child likely to seek repetition of the experience with the man in the new family?
5. Is the child likely to initiate sexual play with other children in the new family?
6. Should there be any physical contact between the new father and the child?
7. What should the attitude of the substitute parents be towards the child's biological family, particularly as many substitute parents feel intensely angry with the abuser and with those who are perceived to have failed in their protection of the child?

Even if some of these issues are not mentioned spontaneously, they should be introduced and explored by the social worker involved with the new family. The new parents may be helped in accepting the child and dealing with their inevitably powerful feelings by watching a video tape of the child's disclosure interview, following which a full expression of their reactions will require support from the professional involved, before discussing the abuse with the child.

Since both the child and her new parents will be aware of the existence and nature of the abuse, it is important that this knowledge is then openly shared. If the person to whom the child made the full disclosure is available, it is often helpful if, in his or her presence, the child tells the new parents about the abuse. The child may need help with this painful task, or may be unwilling to perform it; if so, she should be encouraged to remain present while the information is passed on by the social worker for 'safe keeping' in the new family. Older children in the substitute family, after preparation, could also be present. This process would require repetition if the child should be moved to another family. Only when she has witnessed the acceptance of her story can the child feel free to talk in the new family about her feelings. Thereafter, the initiative should be left to the child, who will progressively experience the comfort of non-critical acceptance. With the passage of time, children in substitute families often recall more details of abusive experiences.

The involvement of other children in the family will depend on their age and maturity, and the parents' wishes. Secrets should, however, be avoided. The abused child will need to know about the extent of awareness of all family members, including the extended family and the new school, in order to feel free from repressed shame and discomfort.

As in other situations of substitute care, the child will wish to retain as many good associations as possible with her family of origin. The abuser and care-givers are best described as misguided and troubled, rather than as bad, although the abuse can never be in any way condoned.

As discussed in relation to protection, new parents should be helped to anticipate possible sexualised behaviour from their new child, and respond by benign vigilance and explanation. Foster parents often find discussion with their social worker of what constitutes normal and acceptable sexual play between children extremely helpful. The most healing experience for a sexually abused child in a new family is acceptance and the experience of physical affection without fear of sexualisation.

Children in residential care

These are often the most troubled children, and their care should follow similar lines to those outlined above. Particular attention is required in the supervision of these children, since the opportunity for repeating sexual experiences is greater, and the children are often difficult to contain.

Staff groups in residential settings require a great deal of support from social workers in their work with these children to enable them to offer co-ordinated and consistent care. The subject of sexual abuse raises a great deal of anxiety for residential staff, some of whom may themselves have been abused. Residential staff are also very vulnerable to sexualised approaches by adolescent, abused children who may seek affection in the only way they know.

7

Therapeutic Intervention

The previous chapter was concerned with defining the aims of professional intervention in child sexual abuse cases, and outlining the issues that characteristically arise when considering a child's long-term needs. In this chapter we discuss the various therapeutic interventions that might be offered to meet these needs, including group work, family therapy, individual counselling or psychotherapy, and work with dyads. Each of these approaches will be discussed separately, concluding with an account of how they might be coordinated. In many cases, it may be a social worker who acts as therapist, for example by running a group or being involved in long-term counselling of a victim of abuse. In other situations, the social worker may refer a child or family on to specialist units, for instance within the child psychiatric service. But in many circumstances it is the social worker who will be co-ordinating the interventions and who will therefore need to be aware of the strengths and limitations of each approach.

Groups

Groups offer particularly suitable settings for helping sexually abused children, their parents and even abusers. This is in large part due to the central defining characteristic of a group, the *collective* aspect, which offers an alternative experience to the isolation, secretiveness and shame that is central to child sexual abuse. For this reason the very act of sharing a regular time with other children or adults who have had similar experiences is likely to afford some emotional relief, in addition to the therapeutic value of the specific content of the group.

Children's groups

Children's groups, because they offer an unprecedented opportunity for openness and support to the most imprisoned participants in the sexually abusive setting, contain considerable potential for helping sexually abused children.

There is a number of variables that may influence the organisation of children's groups. First, there are variations among the children themselves. For example, children joining groups may be living in many different settings: at home with both parents, with the mother alone, in short-term care awaiting a permanent placement, or in a substitute family. Again, the criminal process in relation to the abuser is likely to be at different stages for different children. The nature of the abuse itself and the relationship of the child to the abuser may also produce important differences among potential group members.

In parallel with variations among the children, there can be considerable variability in the content of groups and in the way they are structured, even though their common aim is to enable abused children to meet similarly affected peers. Whatever the particular form of group chosen, however – whether unstructured, activity-centred or focused on emotions or on other specific goals – there are certain features which require specification for a group to be effective. These are listed in Table 7.1, which also presents a suggested checklist for a children's group of a kind which could be run by social workers and others in a variety of settings.

In addition to these general points, there are specific considerations relating to children's groups. These concern the need for a commitment by the child's care-givers, often with support from the assigned social worker, to ensure regular attendance. This considerable commitment would be facilitated by clear lines of communication between group leaders, carers and their social workers, as well as by setting out to meet some of the needs of the carers. An important part of this communication is ensuring the carer's awareness of, and agreement with, the general content of the groups, in particular the sexual education aspect, which often raises questions from the children. Carers who accompany the children usually find much in common with each other, not least the onus of regular attendance and the possible discomfort of having their children involved in an activity from which they are excluded, yet

Table 7.1 *Variables to be defined in group work*

Group leaders	— number, gender
Group structure	— group membership: open or closed
	— age
	— gender
	— number
	— eligibility
	— frequency of meetings
	— duration of meetings
	— duration of group: time-limited or open-ended
Aims	
Format	— structured, unstructured, mixed
Agenda and content of individual sessions	
Process of introduction and ending	
Confidentiality	
Process of recording	
Evaluation	
Supervision	

which is of considerable interest to them. It is likely that the adults will have many common experiences and feelings, including possibly their own abuse, although the concerns of natural and substitute parents differ in many ways. For these reasons, it can be of considerable benefit to form a parallel carers' group, with professional leaders, often social workers. In general, it is likely that the greater the support for the care-givers, the more comfortable and useful the group experience will be for the children.

Group leadership. Group work with sexually abused children is often stressful, with leaders requiring opportunities to share feelings as well as to collaborate in planning, observing and conducting the group. For these reasons, it is advisable to have two group leaders for each group, both of whom should have some experience of work with children.

The question of the suitability of female or male group leaders depends to some extent on whether the group includes boys, girls, or both. In both boys' and girls' groups it is preferable to have at least one female worker, since evocation of male-perpetrated abusive experiences in the presence of two men may be disturbing and difficult for the children. The presence of a man can be particularly helpful in boy's groups, since many abused boys lack experience of a close, non-abusing male figure with whom they can identify. The absence of a meaningful relationship with a non-abusing male may well also be a relevant issue for some sexually abused girls. Furthermore, many of these children lack any experience of relating to a man and a woman who are able to work together in the face of painful feelings. The point here is not to present the heterosexual couple as the only ideal model, but to broaden a child's experience of the kinds of positive relationships that are possible, with the aim of freeing her to make a choice in future relationships of her own.

Finally, a good working relationship between the group leaders is crucial, since the potential for splitting, often inadvertently and unconsciously attempted by the children as a reflection of their own past experiences, is considerable and unhelpful.

Group structure. The group work envisaged here requires a regular membership of no more than eight to ten children, a viable minimum probably being five, which allows for continuity even when inevitable absences occur. Children are best grouped narrowly according to age and maturity, and the content should be adapted accordingly. Appropriate age grouping could be 4–6 years, 7–9 years, 10–12 years, 14–15 years and 16–18 years. Single gender groupings are appropriate, although very young children may be helped in mixed groups where the sharing of sexual information is more open. It is advisable to include more than one child with any particular kind of abusive experience, such as stranger-assault, in order to avoid a situation in which a child may feel isolated from others in the group. Whether siblings who have been abused are best included in the same therapeutic groups depends on several factors. Their age or sex may well determine the need for different groups. When they are close in age and of the same gender, consideration should be given to factors including the similarity of the abusive experiences, the nature of the children's respective relationship with the abuser, and the children's relationship with each other. What is being balanced are the relative advantages of a shared resolution of difficulties versus an opportunity to relate to others as an individual, as well as the capacity of a care-giver to support several children's attendance at different groups and therefore possibly different times.

Continuity is best maintained with weekly meetings, the duration depending on the attention span and therefore maturity of the children. The attention of younger children will only extend to 45–60 minutes, while the older age groups may be able to utilise more than one hour. Time of day must take into consideration the conflicting factors of missing school and tiredness. Good adherence to time limits offers a reassuring and containing experience. The duration of any one group's life will vary with the age of the children. A balance is required between meeting the children's needs and prolonging the label of 'victims', so that for younger children, six to eight weekly meetings are optimal, while groups for older children may continue for several months. Younger children's groups require variety, including structured but active participation by the children in which games, role plays and drawing are particularly useful. It is also important to remember that grouping by gender, age and the facts of sexually abusive experiences nevertheless brings together a collection of children of very widely different social and ethnic backgrounds, intelligence and feelings, and that within the group structure, the equal participation of different group members will require great attention.

Aims, content and process. In broad terms, the aims of group work with sexually abused children fall into four different categories: a) assessment; b) experiential; c) therapeutic; d) educative and preventive.

(a) *Assessment*: the process of arriving at an adequate assessment of a child may be a prolonged one requiring observation over a period of time. The group setting offers an important contribution to this process, one goal being the definition of further needs after the group work is completed. A particular child may, for instance, be observed to be very guilt-ridden or have great difficulty in talking about an area of her experiences. Other children may be isolated within the group or evoke a consistently negative response from others.

(b) *Experience*: the experiential aspect of the group, particularly that of meeting other abused children, is central to its purpose. The realisation that other sexually abused children look like, and are otherwise, ordinary children is extremely reassuring and can help to rectify their frequently stigmatised and tarnished self-image. The mutual support that can be gained, especially by older children, from telling and hearing experiences is considerable, and helps to counteract the strongly internalised injunction to secrecy which is endemic to sexual abuse. In the group, older children can watch the response of peers and adults to the disclosure of their perceived guilt and shame, and witness a lack of the expected disapproval and shock.

(c) *Therapy*: this process begins with the acquisition of a language for sexuality. For younger children this includes the naming of parts of the body and the rudiments of basic anatomy. One way of involving children in this activity is to 'collect' all the possible names which they know for body parts either by calling them out or writing them down anonymously. Consensus can then be reached about words to be used in the group and a distinction made between anatomical and vernacular terminology. Anatomically correct dolls and drawings are helpful here.

Having established a language, older children are then able to move towards talking about their own experiences. Some find this very much harder than others. Group leaders may begin by establishing that all group members know that the children have been subjected to some form of genital or sexual contact with an older person. Some children may experience discomfort in talking openly and therefore the suggestion that children tell each other in pairs is often a safer starting point. The purpose of enabling the children to describe their experiences must not be construed as in any way representing a public exposure of a private, possibly shameful affair. It is in order to dispel the secrecy and particularly to help the children construct an acceptable account of their experiences that this painful exercise is advocated. Many children are burdened by not knowing what to say or how to explain to others the public (as opposed to private) manifestations of the abuse and its disclosure, which include the upset, separations and moves which often follow. The group is seen as providing a safe situation in which to practice this task of giving an account of themselves, which the children are also likely to need when forming future relationships.

The abuser's responsibility for the abuse, the difficulty if not impossibility that the children had faced in attempting to stop and to disclose the abuse, and the rightness of disclosure, can be emphasised and shared. The post-disclosure experiences are usually divergent as well as containing common themes which can be explored. With older children this may lead to further exploration of feelings towards mothers, fathers, abusers and the abuse. The opportunity to learn that aspects of the sexual contact may have been perceived as pleasurable by other children is likely to afford relief. The safe expression of anger is also new to many children. Boys may well be harbouring fears of homosexuality, and a specific discussion of this subject should therefore be included in boys' groups. Finally, acknowledgement of the difficulties faced previously in withstanding the abuse and the new redefinition of where responsibility actually lies, is a prerequisite to arriving at a further and central group task, that of learning to avoid further abuse.

(d) *Prevention and education*: the preventive process begins with arriving at a socially and developmentally appropriate definition of sexuality. All children, more especially those who have been sexually abused, need to learn about qualities of touch which lie along a continuum from good to inappropriate. This is followed by establishing who is allowed to touch various parts of one's body. It is particularly important to match this work to the children's developmental and cognitive stages. The often new experience of learning to cherish and protect one's valued and special parts also helps to raise the very poor self-image which many of the children hold. It leads towards learning new ways of recognising potential abuse and when possible protecting oneself by saying 'no', a response which the abusive relationship clearly did not allow. Children also need to learn about the inappropriateness of keeping secrets where the consequence of divulging them is serious, as opposed to those secrets whose breaching does not greatly matter, but is more akin to a surprise. Children enjoy supplying their own examples. Allied to this is the importance of knowing whom they can tell when someone is attempting to impose a secret on them and identifying the reasons why this had not previously been possible for them.

One aspect of sexual abuse is the premature exposure of children to an incomplete and distorted view of sexuality. It is possible, in a group setting, to introduce a picture of socially acceptable sexuality and reproduction.

Children who have been abused over a period of time may inadvertently behave in ways which are construed as seductive.

Open discussion and recognition of these signals which the children may be giving, and learning alternative ways of relating are particularly suited to a peer group setting. Discussion of what constitutes appropriate peer sexual contact is also valuable and is linked to the notion of privacy The art here is to steer a course which acknowledges both the normality of peer sexual exploration for younger children and activity for older children, alongside the notion of consent by the other, without inducing further guilt. Games can be used to help children recognise when other children are agreeing to or resisting the initiated sexual activity.

It is clear that the various goals listed and considered separately become intertwined in the group process. This agenda is a full one and its implementation requires considerable creativity. It is facilitated by the structured and active participation of the children, and the introduction of light refreshments helps to promote a safe group feeling. In the face of a diverse and full agenda, it is important that some continuity is maintained. Here a pattern of regular opening and closing group activities, designed to promote mutuality, is helpful. Beginnings may be linked to daily life by sharing good and bad news, and meetings may end with mutual compliments. Helping another child to feel good and the experience of being valued for something other than sex are important contributions of the group process. Group leaders' attention to individual needs and feelings can be maintained within the groups by the use of personal notebooks in which children (of an appropriate age) can write short comments, and receive a written response at the following meeting.

Introductions, endings, confidentiality. Children and their carers are often very anxious about joining a group. An initial meeting between the individual child and mother, supported by their social worker, and the group leaders is desirable. This first mutual acquaintance enables the child and mother to voice their questions and concerns and enables the group leaders to hear an outline of the child's experiences. Children are told that the group is offered to sexually abused children and that individual accounts and experiences will only be shared gradually and voluntarily.

The question of confidentiality requires agreement. While group content is confidential to the members, there are occasions when a child divulges information which is considered by the leaders to belong with the protecting adults, or which might usefully be shared with the relevant person in the context of improving family relationships. The child is then encouraged and helped to tell this information or feeling to the appropriate person, outside the group, often in the presence of the group leader. Confidentiality should never override a child's safety.

After the completion of the group, the original individual meeting should be reconvened, and the child's progress and experience reviewed. At this time, further needs which may have been identified during the group process by the leaders could be discussed with the mother or parent and the social worker involved. Examples of such needs may be a recognition of the child's very deep sense of guilt, feelings of great concern for the mother, barely expressed anger at her situation or worryingly sexualised behaviour.

Recording, evaluation and supervision. It is helpful to attempt to define each child's initial requirements from the group and to evaluate the extent to which these have been fulfilled. This process lends a meaningful structure to recording of the group work, in addition to noting the content of individual meetings.

Review and planning are facilitated by a supervisor not involved in the group process. Supervision is additionally time-consuming but is valued by group leaders, offering them an opportunity to step outside the group process and express their own feelings.

Adults' groups

Care-givers' groups. As has already been mentioned, care-givers' groups may evolve naturally alongside children's groups. The adult group formed is a heterogeneous one whose common theme is the care of, and concern for, the sexually abused children – care which is here specifically expressed by facilitating the children's attendance in their group. Membership of such an *ad hoc* group will probably include both foster parents and parents who were the care-givers at the time of the abuse, so that issues surrounding the abuse itself are unlikely to be fully and equally addressed in a way which will be meaningful to all the group participants. Within these constraints, a useful and mutually supportive interchange can still take place.

Mothers' groups. There are many feelings which are likely to be evoked by the sexual abuse of one's own child or children. These feelings can be grouped into: (a) those directed at the abuser, usually of anger, less frequently tinged with ambivalence; (b) concern for the child's experiences and future; (c) guilt for not protecting the child; and (d) discomfort resulting from the disclosure. Many parents' sense of helplessness and low self-esteem may be eased by sharing these feelings with others in similar situations. To this end, social workers may form groups for mothers of abused children, or introduce them to self-help groups. The advantage of a professional-led group is that they are more likely to lead to exploration of individual members' own responsibilities in relation to the abuse, a painful task which may otherwise be avoided. On the other hand, self-help groups in which parents are able to share their experiences and support one another can offer a potent alternative in enhancing the low sense of autonomy that many parents feel in the face of an often considerable professional involvement. This is particularly important for those parents who were themselves abused as children. Indeed, in the process of working in the field of child sexual abuse, a need for therapeutic work with adult victims frequently declares itself.

Groups for substitute parents. Substitute parents find the sharing of problems of receiving sexually abused children into their families particularly helpful. There is often a great deal of anxiety and concern (of the kind described in Chapter 6), and social work support here is of paramount importance to the child. The group setting allows for support of particular parents, the pooling of resourcefulness and professional expertise and the sharing of information.

Groups for abusers. The treatment of abusers is of concern here in its relevance to the future adjustment of the abused child. In this respect, groups for abusers may be helpful in the areas of taking responsibility for the abuse and learning to avoid externalisation of blame. Many abusers also share post-disclosure experiences which often lead them to perceive themselves as victims of society's response to the abuse. Group leaders have an important role to play in sympathetically but firmly resisting this view, which could have destructive effects if later imposed on the victimised child.

Couples including an abuser who wish to maintain a relationship may also join in a group, in which respective responsibilities and relationships are examined.

Families

The extent to which family circumstances and interactions have played a part in the evolution and maintenance of the abusive relationship is an important question in the post-disclosure phase when change is being sought to enable the child to pursue an undisturbed developmental course. The change that is necessary in stranger abuse may occur very soon. At the opposite end of the continuum, incestuous relationships are extremely likely to have become woven into the fabric of family life, and full rehabilitation will entail very intensive therapeutic work, a part of which can be undertaken in a family therapy setting.

Family assessment

Purpose of an assessment. An initial and often brief family assessment is carried out as part of the disclosure process with the immediate aim of determining whether the family's attitude towards the child and the abuse are likely to be both protective and supportive. For a proportion of children it will be considered necessary immediately to seek an alternative, but hopefully temporary, home.

An assessment is likely to be helpful further on in the process for one of two purposes:

1. There may be continuing concerns about the viability of a family in terms of their capacity to meet the child's needs adequately, and a family assessment may be helpful in contributing to the decision-making process. As a result of the assessment, it might be decided that therapeutic work with the family should be attempted.
2. A family may have the intention of remaining together as a unit, but either perceive themselves or be perceived by a professional to be in need of, and likely to benefit from, therapy. For these families an assessment is designed to help in the planning of appropriate work.

There are several family constellations which may be met here:

(a) The family may have decided to exclude the abuser from their midst, or the abuser may not have been living with the family prior to the abuse. The presenting group would therefore not include the abuser but may nevertheless request help.

(b) The family may be planning contact or full rehabilitation with the abuser.

(c) The child may be living in a substitute family, with access to the child's family of origin. The presenting group would then include both the substitute family and those of the original family with whom contact remains.

(d) A substitute family caring for a sexually abused child may be experiencing difficulties in relation to the abused child.

It is important to remember that it may transpire in the course of therapy that the child is not adequately provided for in the family.

The assessment process. A family assessment is a complex process. It seeks to gain a picture of current family functioning as well as some notion of 'myths' or beliefs which may be underpinning the family's way of life. By gaining some knowledge of salient past events in the families of origin of family members as well as in the lifetime of the present family, it is possible to make explanatory links with the family's current belief system (Glaser *et al.*, 1984).

Family functioning may be conceptualised as falling into several component areas comprising: (a) affective status; (b) communication; (c) boundaries; (d) alliances; (e) adaptability-stability; and (f) family competence (Bingley *et al.*, 1984). While a considerable degree of understanding can be derived from interviews with individual family members, a whole-family meeting will usually provide more information in these areas. During a meeting, direct observation of the family, their own reports and the use of a 'circular questioning' approach (Penn, 1982) are all helpful in highlighting relevant aspects of family functioning without making family members feel persecuted.

In the context of child sexual abuse, particular attention should be paid to the following:

1. The degree of emotional warmth and mutual acceptance between family members, particularly in relation to the abused child; conversely, the presence of overt or covert expressions of hostility and scapegoating of family members, particularly of the abused child. The attitude of siblings in this respect is important, since the discomfort felt by them is often blamed on the abused child.

2. The openness of communication or degree of secrecy and veiled communication, particularly in relation to the abuse. The whereabouts and fate of the abuser are examples of subjects which are important to explore.

3. Distance or closeness between family members, particularly between the abused child and the mother, between the parenting couple, between the abuser and mother, and abuser and child (if the abuser is present).

4. The existence or otherwise of clear intergenerational boundaries. Care of younger siblings in the family is one indication of the parental subsystem's functioning. A sibling-like relationship between a parent and a child may indicate a blurring of this boundary.

5. The family's approach to solving problems and response to crises; specifically, the response to the sexual abuse of one or more of the children in terms of the degree of problem resolution or avoidance, and holding of responsibility within the family as opposed to externalisation and scapegoating. The extent of awareness and acknowledgement of other problems in the family (if they exist).

6. In exploring aspects of the family's history, it is possible both to seek links between the present and the past, and to gain a clinical impression of family members' capacity to reflect and join in the link-making process. Indications of sexual abuse in the families of origin are particularly relevant. An account of the current family's history may also point to the family's position along a continuum which ranges from a disorganised extreme, and continues through flexibility and stability towards a rigid pattern at the other extreme.

All family members who are considered to be part of the current or proposed unit, or all those likely to have access to the child, should be invited, alongside all social workers and other professionals involved with the child and family, including probation officers (if applicable). The family's response in bringing whoever they choose, forms part of the assessment. For example, the exclusion of siblings might indicate continuing secrecy within the family. Detailed introductions, including surnames, form a useful starting point and naturally lead to an account of previous marriages or different fathers for the children. Family members' stated agenda for the meeting is one indication of motivation. Encouraging the family to give an account of the abuse and of their perception of the disclosure process and its consequences is a helpful means of gaining an understanding of the family. It will also serve as an indication of the family members' current position in relation to responsibility for the abuse. Other helpful aspects to explore may be family members' own explanation for difficulties which they perceive, and their own attempted solutions to these difficulties. Enquiring about what would have to be different for the family to be free of professional involvement/interference may highlight the degree of awareness of unresolved issues as well as the attitude to and co-operation with the professional network.

This assessment, whilst possibly therapeutic in shedding light on certain relationships and interactions, is not part of family therapy. The assessment may suggest the direction which the therapeutic endeavour might take. This is likely to include work with individuals, dyads and the whole family, if it is deemed that the child's needs will continue to be met in that setting. The assessment may thus become part of the decision-making process and contribute to statutorily supported outcomes. As part of this process, it is often helpful to gauge the family's capacity for change by use of limited contracts over a number of sessions. It is important that the assessment function of the work is made clear to families who might otherwise feel betrayed by what they perceive to be a treatment process.

Family therapy

Therapeutic work with the whole family group is one of the treatment modalities which may be offered following the assessment. There are certain specific issues which particularly lend themselves to family therapy.

Secrecy. The resolution of the problem of secrecy can ultimately only occur with open communication. It may well be necessary for preparatory work to be done with individuals or dyads. Parents' wishes to withhold full information, especially from siblings, must initially be respected if a therapeutic alliance is to be maintained, even if it is felt not to be in the family's long-term interest. There are several useful steps in dealing with secrets. In establishing who does and does not know certain facts, it is often possible to demonstrate that more is known by those believed to be ignorant than was thought. This applies particularly to younger siblings of abused children. Frequently, a child reveals full awareness of supposedly secret areas in reponse to relatively straightforward enquiries about what they might know about them – for example, father's whereabouts (prison) or the reasons for an abused child's residence away from home. If it becomes apparent that certain family members, who may include important people in the immediate extended family, are genuinely uninformed, it is usually only possible to overcome the secrecy by directly addressing the anxieties that maintain it. This work may well have to be carried out with the holders of the secret on their own. Secrets are often maintained either for the supposed protection of the one(s) in the dark, for fear of a negative reaction in response to enlightenment or because the holder(s) of the secret feels unable to find a way of breaking it. Exploration of these concerns, anxieties or fears often leads to their diminution. Holders of the secret, often the parents, often greatly appreciate specific and explicit guidance on the way to breach the secret. A family session may be used for divulgence. Some families prefer, after preparation, to talk more openly in the privacy of their home. In that case it is important for the therapist to witness a change in communication at a later meeting. This change would be indicated by the family's ability to talk openly about the previously avoided subjects.

Sexuality. This is allied to secrets and openness of communciation. Often a modelling approach by a therapist who shows willingness to talk about sexuality is valuable in enabling the subject to be mentioned. The therapist can explore the family's language and names for sexual organs and activities, and initiate a process in which sexuality, of which all are individually aware, can be talked about more openly within the family. The style and language should be related to the children's respective ages and maturity, and openness must not go beyond a point which is acceptable to the parents.

Siblings. The integration of siblings into the family's adjustment process is an important issue, both for their own and the abused child's welfare. In the absence of an opportunity to express their feelings and receive adequate and accurate explanations, siblings often continue to harbour fear or resentment against a parent or the abused child. This therapeutic process is likely to proceed over a period of time and might include work during the session, particularly in enabling siblings to speak and be listened to. In addition, parents often appreciate guidance in continuing this process at home.

Intergenerational boundaries and family organisation. These concepts are often relevant to families in which a child, by the fact of being sexually abused, may have crossed an intergenerational boundary. There may be other manifestations of the same phenomenon, and family therapy can be helpful in re-establishing the rights and responsibilities of children and parents. These may include the right of children to be looked after instead of looking after parents or younger siblings. They also include the right of parents to their own temporal and private space. Some parents who themselves suffer low self-esteem require and appreciate support and help in establishing their position in the family, often having previously felt too guilty or unequal to the tasks of setting appropriate boundaries. This aspect of the work in particular is fruitfully enacted in family sessions, a necessary prerequisite to attempting change at home without the support of the therapist.

Scapegoating and responsibility. Although deeply ingrained attitudes towards individuals may require individual work, family settings are important in marking changes, which often emerge during a family session. The previously scapegoated child may well require help in accepting a new view of herself by the family, and this mutual process of adjustment requires the presence of all the family members. A child may thus, for instance, expect to be met with a critical response, the absence of which may go unnoticed unless brought to the child's attention.

It is unreasonable to expect an individual to take the first steps towards assuming responsibility for abuse in public. Initially this work is more appropriately done with individuals. However, an open statement of responsibility by an abuser is one of the most important steps in therapy. This again is a mutual process, since individual family members' responses, such as accepting the abuser's new position by seeking to protect him and lighten his load or conversely continuing to reject him, will determine future relationships within the family. The question of full rehabilitation of a family within which abuse has occurred, remains an open one. There are considerable doubts about the possibility of desexualising relationships and of bringing about sufficient change in relationship patterns to ensure unequivocal safety for children. These doubts do not in any way invalidate the importance of a full and relatively public assumption of responsibility

Other family problems. Other difficulties may have emerged during the assessment or treatment process which are only indirectly related to the abuse or are independent of it. These may include behaviour problems experienced by siblings, relationship issues or unresolved past experiences such as losses affecting the whole family. Family patterns such as rigidity are likely to lead to difficulty in responding to externally imposed or internally generated changes, such as occur during the natural stages of growing up and the family life-cycle. These may well be explored within family therapy, as may patterns of disorganisation, which often require the introduction of a degree of structure before an exploration of the causes can fruitfully begin.

Individual therapy

Any individual closely involved in the abusive relationship may require individual work.

Children

Alongside, after or in the absence of a time-limited group experience, many sexually abused children require individual contact with a professional, usually their social worker, teacher or counsellor. This contact may be a regular one or alternatively the person may be available for the child to consult when in need. One of the central components of this work is the continuity which the counsellor offers the child over a long period of time. Children may harbour anxieties about their bodies and their sexuality over many years, especially in puberty. There may be periods of sadness and guilt. Renewed contact with the abuser is often a point of crisis, anxiety or occasionally excitement during which the child is likely to require support and guidance. The presence of a long-term social worker who might, for instance, span changes of home and family, can enable a child to express feelings of sadness and happiness, or likes and dislikes about their alternative carers. Social workers in this role can also help a child maintain contact with her extended family. Very importantly, they may ease the child's sense of being a 'sexual abuse victim' by carrying with them knowledge of the details of the abuse, lessening the child's burden of having to repeat their story to new care-givers. In all this it is important that the long-term counselling role is not perceived by the child or her care-giver as substitute parenting. It is the relative independence from and addition to the parenting task that contributes to the child's emotional well-being.

It is likely that children involved in a long-standing, incestuous relationship will also require more intensive work, often directed at easing a deep sense of guilt, responsibility, defilement, ambivalence and unexpressed or inappropriately directed anger. This may also apply to those children who perceive their move to an alternative family as a rejection, although here the individual work must often await decisions on the child's permanent home.

Intensive individual psychotherapy entails the formation of an important relationship with a therapist, which usually continues for some time. It is likely that the work with the child will focus not only on the abuse and sexuality, but also on other experiences, relationships and the child's view of herself. As the work progresses, children often pass through a phase when many negative frightening and angry feelings emerge. The child may at that point resist meeting the therapist. For the process to be helpful to the child, a great deal of firm support may then be needed to allow for resolution of these conflicts to occur. For these reasons, the child will need the full commitment and constant support which only a secure home can provide. It is unwise to commence pyschotherapy, only to discontinue it for very important geographical reasons when the child is placed with a suitable family. The child's secure position in a family takes precedence over psychotherapeutic needs. Psychotherapy may only occasionally be considered to be part of a preparatory process for permanent placement and be thought important enough to delay such a move. Sometimes a psychotherapeutic relationship may span across a planned move from a temporary to a permanent home.

Mothers

Some mothers request individual psychotherapeutic help, most often when they are feeling deeply beset by guilt or to help deal with the effects of abuse that they themselves may have suffered in childhood. In the main, there is an important role for social workers in providing supportive counselling or, sometimes, educative work to help a mother assume an autonomous parental role (particularly if the abuser was previously in the family), to raise low self-esteem, and to deal with the many stresses of the difficult post-disclosure period. In the choice which the caretaking parent may have to face between the abuser (who could be her father, son, husband or cohabitee) and the child, the most painful and difficult decisions are called for. Other parents will require a great deal of protection from the abuser, who may try to insist on maintaining contact against the caretaking parent's wishes. the difficult task of examining what possible part the mother may have played in allowing the abuse to occur can usually only be undertaken in private. An altered view of the child's part in the abuse, which may previously have been regarded as seductive and possibly usurping of the mother's position, will hopefully follow.

Further work may be required in helping mothers to understand their child's premature sexual arousal, which may lead to masturbation or to a search for repetition leading to a need for extra protection, particularly from new cohabitees. This work with the caretaking parent, usually carried out by a social worker, is often one of the central therapeutic tasks. It may be difficult and slow, but for many children it will determine the viability of continued care in their natural family.

Abusers

All abusers have undoubted individual needs, which are not by any means always acknowledged. The first step, without which no therapy can reasonably be expected to lead to change, is for the fact of sexual contact to be admitted. In order for this contact to be seen as abusive to the child, the abuser must accept full responsibility for it. So long as the child's apparent agreement with, possible enjoyment of, or even perceived invitation to the sexual contact is continued to be put forward in mitigation of the abuser's resposibility, he cannot fully accept the abusive nature of the contact. Only when this is achieved can he truly apologise to the child (an experience all too rarely offered to children) and be in a position to benefit from therapy. In seeking to achieve this progression for the abuser, it is helpful to address the anxieties that underlie the abuser's denial, helping him feel supported in facing his worst fears. Quite apart from the obvious fear of conviction, the more personal pain is that of having to live with one's own deeds and responsibility for them. This may lead to depression and possibly suicidal thoughts. Occasionally, suicide is the actual outcome – which is certainly an almost intolerable burden for an abused child to carry. Much of this work is likely to require an individual-therapy setting, since a private acknowledgement is likely to precede a public one in a group of abusers. Even with such acknowledgement, the success of therapeutic work is as yet difficult to predict reliably. Those abusers whose activity is related to alcohol abuse may benefit from help with the latter. Behavioural, psychotherapeutic and group approaches have their place and are not mutually exclusive.

There has been much debate about the possibility of carrying out effective therapeutic work under legal compulsion, such as a probation order with treatment. This is the most desirable sentence for most child sexual abusers. Based on reports on work carried out in the USA (e.g. Giaretto 1977, 1981), it appears to be possible to combine treatment and compulsion successfully; in the absence of a safe alternative, there is good reason to adopt similar approaches in this country. Probation officers, in conjunction with clinical psychologists, forensic psychiatrists and psychotherapists are the most likely professionals to offer help to abusers. Those abusers sentence to custody may receive help in some prisons, although others will receive only protection from fellow inmates.

Dyads

Within the various dyadic relationships in the family, the most conflicting and painfully unresolved mutual feelings are likely to be harboured. These dyads include particularly the non-abusing parent and child; child and abuser; and parent and abuser. The initial exploration of these feelings is often best undertaken with the individuals concerned either on their own or in group settings, before bringing the two protagonists together.

The tasks for therapeutic work with the significant dyads have been outlined in Chapter 6. The mother–child dyad presents the most important technical problems for social workers and other professionals. Bridging the distance that may have arisen between mother and child and enabling each to learn about and comprehend the feelings of the other is a process that can be substantially helped by the presence of an outsider or, preferably, two workers who can take up supportive positions with respect to the individual participants, while aiming to avoid mutual recriminations. For the professionals involved it is important to maintain neutrality, remembering nevertheless that however difficult the parent's task and experience has been, it is the child who is the dependent one in this unequal relationship. Indeed, there is a danger that the child may return to a parental and protective position. This dyadic work is aimed at restoring a parent–child relationship, rather than meeting the parent's needs, which are likely to emerge clearly and may well highlight the necessity for further individual support.

Where the carer and the abuser intend to continue a relationship, very careful work will be required, particularly if full rehabilitation is being contemplated. As described in Chapter 6, a formal renegotiation of roles and of the status of the relationship is required, whether to support the mother in assuming more control, or to dissolve the relationship in a way that deals appropriately with the emotional welfare of the children. If carer and abuser are remaining together, a central issue to deal with in therapy will be their sexual relationship, which is likely to have been mutually dissatisfying or conflict-ridden. This may mean that there is a need for specific psychosexual counselling, and social workers should consider referral to specialist agencies accordingly.

Some abuser–carer relationships (such as father–daughter or brother–sister) have a long history prior to the abuse of the child and may have been sexualised. Lack of resolution of the feelings generated by such relationships is likely to affect the child adversely. Dyadic work here may be valuable, although it is likely that considerable prior support and preparation of the individuals involved will be required.

The main purpose of abuser–child dyadic contact in a therapeutic setting is for the abuser clearly to accept responsibility for the abuse and to receive the child's feelings without generating guilt in her.

Such occasions need very careful preparation with substantial individual work with the abuser being an essential part of this preparation. As described earlier, it may be the case that family sessions provide a more appropriate forum for abuser–child contact, and social workers should be wary of separating off the abuser and child from other family members.

The co-ordination of a therapeutic approach

From what has been written it will be clear that no single form of therapy is likely to serve all the child's and family members' needs at all stages of the post-disclosure process. Different modalities and therapeutic groupings complement each other, and the work often depends on progress in one area leading to continuation in another. For example, when individual help for a mother enables her to alter her view of the child's role in the abusive relationship, it is important to bring mother and child together so that this development may be communicated directly between mother and child. When secrets or mystifications are evident from work with abused children or their siblings, planning for a whole family meeting in which openness is encouraged could be the next step. Conversely, family, group or dyadic work may highlight particular painful issues for individuals and it may be clinically evident that work with that individual on her or his own is required before interpersonal issues can be reactivated. Another aspect of this therapeutic interdependence is reflected in decisions about a child's readiness to join a group. Questions concerning the child's sense of guilt, self-blame and acknowledgement of powerlessness in relation to the abuser as well as details of the abuse, require exploration with the child on her own first. It is only when retrospective reassurance has begun to be established that the child will be emotionally receptive to forward-looking preventive work. The younger the child and the shorter the period of abuse, the briefer the period of individual work dealing specifically with the sexual abuse is likely to be. However, there may be other major problems that require longer-term work.

The principle that lies behind co-ordination of the various therapeutic modes is the constant tension between and interdependence of personal intrapsychic feelings and the expression of feelings within relationships. The art lies in the temporal co-ordination of these various aspects while preserving the confidential boundaries required for therapeutic work to proceed. It is therefore important that responsibility for co-ordination rests with a named individual, usually the social worker, who is aware of progress in the therapeutic work and is able to keep informed all those who are professionally involved. This includes the child's school, who need to be sufficiently well informed to support the child and any treatment she may be receiving.

One of the key factors in determining the content and direction of therapeutic work is the stage of the post-disclosure process that has been reached. The sequence, constituent points and actual stage varies from child to child. For instance, the issues for a child whose family is awaiting the remanded father's decision about pleading guilty or not guilty are very different from those of a child whose divorced parents are in dispute over access, the father having denied the allegations. A boy who has been abused by his maternal grandfather as another victim of a long-standing, incestuously active old man, will face different difficulties from a girl whose abuser reappears after release from gaol. The problem of having to protect children from abusers who continue to deny the abuse is a difficult one, and may continue over a number of years. Abuse which only comes to light after the child settles in an alternative family requires none of the domestic and often traumatic crisis work associated with acute stranger assaults, although these abused children are likely to benefit from a therapeutic response directed at the effects of the abuse on the child's social behaviour, self-esteem and sexuality.

Therapeutic needs are not only related to the stage of the process, but are also closely influenced by the child and family's response to the professional network's activity. The placing of a child's name on a child abuse register may be construed as protecting or persecuting, as may be the appointment of a named social worker. Particularly strong feelings are evoked by police and legal activity. Police decisions not to prosecute may increase the child's feelings of guilt and sense of not being believed. In the extended family's eyes it may be cited as a verdict of not guilty. A custodial sentence may increase the child's guilt further or it may give the family a breathing-space which allows work to continue. This can now include the abuser in prison joining marital or family work. A suspended sentence often evokes anger from all but the abuser.

Each one of these moves by outside agencies will be incorporated into family members' feelings towards each other. In cases of stranger abuse where the abuser disappears or the evidence is deemed insufficient to lead to prosecution, the child and family are left frightened and angry. Meanwhile, long-standing relationships and feelings continue to run deep.

In summary, the basic issues may be repeated. Every sexually abused child will require some help in relation to the sexual nature of the abuse, protective aspects often being well suited to group work.

Questions of guilt and responsibility are likely to arise in most cases. The closer the relationships in the triangle between abuser, child and care-giver, the more painful and difficult the issues. They are likely to require individual, group, dyadic and family work.

Separations may be required for the protection of the child. Those involving a move for the child rather than the abuser are likely to be perceived as rejections by the child. Those requiring departure by the abuser may place the care-giving parent in deep conflict. Separations may be temporary or permanent, and at any given point the stage reached in the decision-making process has a direct bearing on the nature of therapeutic work.

Families of, and children who are, victims of abuse from outside the family require support and reassurance.

Substitute parents have special needs related to their particular tasks in caring for a child whose previous traumata are likely to have been outside their sphere of experience and involvement.

The legal decisions concerning prosecution, evidence and sentencing carry very significant implications for the child and the family. The successful treatment of abusers remains an unresolved issue.

8

Professional and Team Issues

Emotional issues: impact and responses

Each one of the words 'child sexual abuse' is a source of strong emotional responses. Issues pertaining to children tend to involve protective feelings, which are often heightened in those who work with children in distress. These feelings can become particularly acute when, as in many cases of sexual abuse, the child has been exploited by an adult with responsibility for her well-being. In addition, especially when carrying out investigative interviews, many social workers are disturbed by the thought that they may be perceived by the child as another abuser and that they may be doing more harm to the child, even though their motives are the best. This is especially the case if the interviewer is a man: the parameters of the abusive situation may feel uncomfortably close to what is going on in the disclosure interview (man 'abusing' child by exploring her sexuality and sexual experiences – see Frosh, 1987b).

Sexuality arouses excitement, embrarrassment, confusion or inhibition in most adults; this is complicated for professionals by the additional factor of having to deal with a child's sexual experiences. For example, a social worker interviewing a child may be disturbed by her or his awareness of feelings of excitement or disgust at the child's description of what has happened to her – which may include descriptions of sexual experiences that the social worker has never had. Being aware of these feelings whilst avoiding imposition or projection of them on to the child is a difficult art that demands a considerable amount of personal insight and honesty. Similarly, the abuse often activates anger, indignation or retribution, as well as a wish to rescue the victim. The fact that in this form of abuse the abuser is predominantly male, produces further emotional responses and has differential implications for female and male workers. For men, there may be a sense of collective guilt or alternatively defensiveness, either of which is liable to cloud the view of issues pertaining to a particular child or family. For instance, there may be an unarticulated wish on the part of a male worker to make up for the abuser's guilt, producing ineffectual rescue attempts or making it impossible for the child to express any ambivalent feelings she may have. Other men may regard the child as unduly sexually provocative, or they may harbour feelings of censure about the mother's emotional or sexual unavailability.

One response to the sexual abuse of children is to adopt a strongly anti-men stance. Although men are responsible for child sexual abuse, a simple conceptual division between men as aggressors and women as victims makes it more difficult to perceive and address the issues that arise when dealing with the effects of abuse. For example, a strongly anti-men stance may interfere with a worker's ability to tolerate a child's ambivalence towards the abuser, as well as inadvertently standing in the way of understanding the mother's positive or negative contribution towards the evolution of the abuse. This is especially so if the mother was herself abused in childhood and is viewed in the victim role. It may raise particular difficulties for an assigned social worker with statutory responsibility that is aimed at protecting the child. Such statutory involvement carries with it an implied statement of mistrust of the parent's ability to provide adequate care for the child. For a social worker wishing to support an abused mother at the same time as carrying statutory responsibility for the children, a conflict may arise. This can only be resolved by recognising that from the child's point of view, a parent is regarded as a protector and care-giver, not as a victim.

With the high prevalence of sexual abuse, it is inevitable that some professionals will themselves have been abused in childhood. Although this may heighten the worker's sensitivity to a child's needs, feelings about one's own sexual abuse may be sufficiently powerful or unresolved to lead, for instance, to strong identification with the child or overwhelming anger with the abuser. Whilst these feelings are in themselves understandable, they can interfere with the task of meeting the particular child's needs. It is sometimes only in the context of working with children who have been sexually abused that professionals begin to recognise, share and deal with their own past experiences; for this reason, it is important that institutional responses to child sexual abuse include the provision of emotionally supportive supervision arrangements.

There are other sources of stress arising out of work in this area. One of these is the frequent experience of being faced with conflicting accounts given by child and abuser and sometimes by the mother. The disagreements may centre around the nature, frequency and age of onset of the abuse, or in their most disturbing form may arise as an allegation by one which is totally denied by the other. The need to respond to such denial in a therapeutic as opposed to condemnatory manner, so that the disclosure is advanced rather than prevented, is in practice very difficult. A further source of stress is the increasing disclosure rate. Referral criteria based on clear indications of interference with a child's mental and emotional health would by themselves yield a great amount of child sexual abuse work. The additional concept of human rights, in this case the rights of children not to be sexually abused regardless of the degree of potential emotional damage which the abuse may cause to any individual child, further increases the load. In addition, the legal/ethical definition of abuse does not allow for discrimination of individual clients' needs; it may, therefore, at times force social workers to intervene in a way which they perceive as more harmful than the abuse, yet which they are not able to avoid. As the volume of work increases, there is also a pressure to continue to respond positively to new referrals, which are perceived as crises, rather than to continue the painstaking long-term work which may be required with an existing case load.

The emotional responses to which child sexual abuse gives rise are in practice usually positively harnessed. If recognised and respected, the concern, protectiveness and even the anger felt by professionals can generate an energy which produces a productive approach to the needs of children and families. Therapeutically, awareness of the multiplicity of feelings which sexual matters arouse allows for a sensitive and respectful approach to a child, listening for and acknowledging the variety of responses which the child may have, rather than seeking to impose assumptions about uniformly negative reactions. Initial and understandable wishes to punish the abuser can be translated into more productive avenues which seek to help him assume responsibility and to face the consequences, as well as perhaps to seek therapy. More generally, those advances that have been achieved in child protective legislation have come about in response to the strong emotions produced by the plight of children, translated into statutory terms and often backed by legal orders and the power of the courts.

The central skill of those working in the field of human relations is to convert their own sensitivity and understanding into a response which is helpful to the particular patient or client. It is for this reason that child sexual abuse work cannot be carried out by an isolated professional; it requires consultation with others. Only by increasing one's self-awareness through supportive supervision and peer discussion can one guard against the danger of an unprocessed and unaware emotional response which is unlikely to meet the needs of the child or family. Furthermore, in a situation of clearly insufficient professional resources, it requires a team to reach decisions about priorities.

The division of labour: interprofessional relationships

Throughout the complex series of events that surround the uncovering of child sexual abuse, the social worker is likely to be centrally situated and to be the professional who is in closest contact with the family. However, child sexual abuse work usually involves a variety of agencies and services, both sequentially and in parallel. The actions of each member of the professional network will depend on the nature of a previous member's involvement, and will have a significant bearing on another's subsequent work. The interprofessional dependence is even more acute when different services are simultaneously involved. This may lead to feelings of interprofessional rivalry or co-operation and relief, depending on the degree of clarity of respective functions and on an understanding of the aims and methods used by different agencies.

Avoidance of interprofessional rivalry is a critical issue in work as complex as this. Unfortunately, there is a number of features of child sexual abuse work which promote such rivalry, in addition to the simple difficulty of containing the powerful emotions that sexual abuse provokes. For instance, each of the stages described above may be perceived by family members as stressful or traumatic, and a natural response is to complain about one professional or agency's involvement to another. Indeed, at times there may be agreement with the family's view, complicating the issue of interprofessional co-operation.

It is sometimes the case that a particular professional may become identified with the position and well-being of one family member. For example, a social worker might see her or his primary responsibility as being the protection of the child, while the general practitioner may be particularly aware of the mother's predicament, especially if this is expressed in somatic symptoms. A health visitor or teacher may be concerned with the welfare of a sibling in the midst of the family's turmoil, while a probation officer might be attempting to represent the abuser's position. A situation may then arise in which professional disagreement develops, often ostensibly relating to practical issues such as access arrangements or need for, and frequency of, therapy. What may be inadvertently acted out is not a true interprofessional disagreement, but a conflict by proxy (Furniss, 1983), in which the unresolved family members' differences and feelings are being expressed on their behalf by professionals. Avoidance of this unhelpful but understandable situation can only be achieved through regular interprofessional meetings, in which there is a clarification, review and redefinition of respective roles.

One particularly difficult problem of professional role is the position of a social worker charged with the task of meeting the needs of both the child and the mother, especially when conflicts of interest and feelings exists between them. In this situation another professional should be brought in, such as a psychiatric social worker or psychotherapist from a child psychiatric agency. Quite apart from the relief which the sharing of therapeutic and protective tasks can bring to the professionals involved, there are specific benefits for the family. These lie in the modelling experience gained from observation of co-operation and conflict-resolution between professionals representing different family members. The success of the collaboration, however, will depend on clear communication between the social worker and the other professional.

The question of confidentiality reflects awareness of the importance of individuals in the midst of complex inter-agency involvement. In advocating open communication between professionals, it is well to remember that individual family members have a right to privacy, and indeed its absence will stand in the way of the necessary therapeutic work. This delicate balance calls for careful judgement in discriminating between that information which has a bearing on others' well-being and those feelings whose nature does not require, or is indeed inappropriate, to be shared. Some of the difficulties in deciding what to share and what to retain within the relationship with the client may be resolved in discussion with the client. Indeed, good practice dictates that family members should at least know what information is to be shared among professionals, even if they may not agree with this. The latter situation is most likely to occur when a child's safety is at issue.

The special position of the social worker

The position of the social worker as central to the management of child sexual abuse cases, especially in their co-ordination and child protection aspects, has been explicit throught Part II of this book. Only a few summary points need to be made here. Even if a social worker is not the person suspecting abuse or receiving a partial disclosure, Social Services will be informed on a duty basis. In the case of a partial disclosure, where the child's word is accepted as *prima facie* evidence of abuse, a social worker, together with the police, will initiate and pursue the investigation of what has happened, the family circumstances and relationships surrounding the child, and questions of appropriate immediate protection. This is likely to include the setting up of a disclosure interview, which is most appropriately conducted conjointly by a trained social worker and police officer. It may also be at this time that the first and crucial contact will be made with the child's care-givers or mother. The social worker may accompany the child to the medical examination. At the subsequent case conference an assessment of the safety of children in the family, as well as a plan for protection and therapy, will rely to a considerable extent on information gained by the social worker, under the same well-established procedure accepted for physical child abuse.

As has been outlined in Chapters 6 and 7, the task of child protection which falls on the social worker, particularly when accompanied by statutory requirements, is a very complex one, raising the question of the feasibility of combining a legal and therapeutic role. If the child's safety is deemed to require statutory support, the family and social worker enter into a required relationship, the existence of which is not in the power of either party, but rather in the hands of the court, or of the child abuse legislation. Although viewing the social worker's position in this light may seem to render her or him powerless, it can become a liberating context. It enables the social worker to be freed from becoming the target for potential attack or rejection by the family, and allows the social worker to join with the family in working towards a common goal, namely, the dissolution of their required relationship. The social worker's task becomes redefined as seeking to enable the family to convince society that the children's needs are now being adequately met within the family and no longer require outside surveillance. The social worker thus temporarily becomes part of the therapeutic system.

It is clear from all that has been said that social workers who are key workers in this field require support, supervision and a recognition from within their own hierarchy of the heavy burden which child sexual abuse cases impose.

The place of specialist child sexual abuse teams

Specialist teams dealing with child sexual abuse have evolved in some areas. The impetus has arisen from child psychiatric and paediatric agencies, initially in the USA and later in Britain (see, Giaretto, 1981; Furniss *et al.*, 1984), with team members quickly gaining expertise as a result of working with the many referrals with which they found themselves flooded. It is this intense involvement with large numbers of cases over a relatively short period of time that has produced current patterns of therapeutic responses and techniques of interviewing

It is now widely agreed that investigative and disclosure work is best carried out conjointly by specifically trained area social workers and police officers. It is, however, likely that specialist teams, emanating from different settings such as child guidance and child psychiatric clinics, Social Services and voluntary social work agencies, will contine to have an important role to perform. There are three main aspects to this work: consultative, therapeutic and teaching. With difficult problems, a professional who is not directly involved can be helpfully consulted by a group of professionals who are, if the consultant is well versed with procedure and experienced in working with sexually abused children. It is sometimes easier to hold a systemic view of a problem from without than from within the system. Some of the long-term therapeutic work, be it with individuals, dyads, whole families or groups, requires more specialist skills as well as the peer supervision and support which a team provides. Much of the training and teaching in child sexual abuse work is currently undertaken by members of specialist teams, and it is likely that this function will continue.

Training and practice development

Locally based multidisciplinary groups are increasingly being formed with the task of evolving local practice guidelines, identifying the professionals to be involved, defining training needs, and overseeing their fulfilment. It is vital that these groups continue as local forums for increasing mutual understanding and trust between agencies who have not always shared common views, aims or practices. These groups include representatives from Social Services, police, paediatrics, child psychiatry, community health, family practitioner and probation services. Some issues are procedural and some require the acquisition of new skills such as interviewing a child and the medical examination of sexually abused children. Others call for the application of recognised child protective and therapeutic practices to newly defined problems. The fulfilment of these training needs is likely to pose a sizeable challenge and require considerable resources if the requirements of professionals are to be met.

Conclusion

This chapter has focused on the difficult personal and professional issues that face social workers and others dealing with children who have been sexually abused. As such, it links with our major argument in this book: that child sexual abuse is a social phenomenon of considerable complexity, having its roots in socialisation factors, its manifestations in interpersonal and systemic processes, and its effects in durable internal distress and trans-generational disturbances. For those professionals working with sexually abused children and their families, every case brings new problems. For social workers in particular, who carry the burden of statutory responsibility for children's protection and who have such a central role in attempts to repair the damage that abuse causes, this work is among the hardest that can be envisaged. It is our hope that the guidelines for practice given in Part II will have clarified the lines of action available and appropriate to each case, and will be a source of ideas for constructive interventions. This will only suffice, however, when combined both with good training and with continuing supervisory guidance and professional and personal support.

Guide to Further Reading

Chapter 1   Myth and Reality: The Dimensions of Child Sexual Abuse

The best overview of statistics on child sexual abuse is provided by Finkelhor (1984). There are also useful accounts of the prevalence and effects of child sexual abuse in D. Finkelhor (ed.) *A Sourcebook on Child Sexual Abuse* (London, Sage, 1986). The studies by Baker and Duncan (1985) and Russell (1983) are worth reading in their entirety. Over the past few years, the journal *Child Abuse and Neglect* has published numerous articles on child sexual abuse, many of which deal with its characteristics and statistical distribution.

Chapter 2   A Multi-faceted Phenomenon: Sexuality and Child Sexual Abuse

Finkelhor (1984) is again a good source for a thoughtful view on the aetiology of child sexual abuse. Jackson (1982) supplies an interesting description of sexual socialisation, whilst a more strongly feminist account can be found in Ward (1984), which also contains some striking personal testimonies. The literature on masculine sexuality is unsatisfactory, but a provocative collection of essays can be found in A. Metcalf and M. Humphries (eds) *The Sexuality of Men* (London, Pluto Press, 1985). For a description of psychoanalytic theories and of feminist reappraisals, see Frosh (1987a).

Chapter 3   A Family Affair?

CIBA (1984) is the most influential family-systems-based account of child sexual abuse, but provides very little theory. The interviews around which Herman (1981) is written are moving and revealing of family processes. For a critical analysis of family ideology see M. Barrett and M. McIntosh, *The Anti-social Family* (London, Verso, 1982).

163

Chapter 4   Suspicion and Disclosure: Initial Professional Responses

The recommendations for professional practice to be found in CIBA (1984) have been important in influencing the policy of many local authorities and should be read in the light of the more detailed guidelines provided here.

Chapter 5   The Process of Validation and Decision-making

The best available description of the validation interview and of the issues to be considered when interpreting the information received from children is that of Jones and McQuiston (1985). This brief pamphlet is a concise but sophisticated guide through a very difficult area of work. For further accounts of the assessment and treatment process, see A. Bentovim, A. Elton, J. Hidlebrand, M. Tranter and E. Vizard, *Child Sexual Abuse within the Family – Assessment and Treatment* (London, John Wright, 1988).

Chapter 6   After Validation: The Aims of Further Professional Involvement

In addition to the relevant chapters in the Bentovim *et al.* book mentioned above, T. Simmons, *Child Sexual Abuse: An Assessment Process* (London, National Society for the Prevention of Cruelty to Children, 1986), contains much useful material.

Chapter 7   Therapeutic Intervention

There is an enormous literature on the different therapeutic approaches described here, but little of it pertains directly to child sexual abuse. Again, the volume by Bentovim *et al.* (1988) mentioned above attempts to rectify the situation, although its emphasis is on family interventions.

Chapter 8   Professional and Team Issues

See Furniss (1983) and Dale *et al.* (1986) for accounts of how professional teams can 'mirror' the disturbed functioning of sexually abusive families.

References

Abel, G. Barlow, D., Blanchard, E, and Guid, D, (1977) 'The Components of Rapists' Sexual Arousal', *Archives of General Psychiatry*, 34, pp. 895–903.

Baker, A. and Duncan, S. (1985) Child Sexual Abuse: A Study of Prevalence in Great Britain', *Child Abuse and Neglect*, 9, pp. 457–67.

Benward, J. and Densen-Gerber, J. (1975) 'Incest as a Causative Factor in Anit-Social Behaviour', *paper presented at the American Academy of Forensic Sciences*, in Finkelhor, 1984.

Bingley, L., Loader, P. and Kingston, W. (1984) 'Further Development of a Format for Family Description', *Australian Journal of Family Therapy*, 5, pp. 215–18.

Chodorow, N. (1978) *The Reproduction of Mothering*, Berkeley, University of California Press.

Christie, M., Marshall, W. and Lanthier, R. (1978) 'A Descriptive Study of Incarcerated Rapists and Paedophiles', *Canadian Penitentiary Services*, in Langevin, 1985.

CIBA Foundation (1984) *Child Sexual Abuse within the Family*, London, Tavistock.

Conte, J. and Berliner, L. (1987) 'The Impact of Sexual Abuse on Children: Clinical Findings', in L. Walker (ed.) *Handbook on Sexual Abuse of Children: Assessment and Treatment Issues*, New York, Springer.

Dale, P., Waters, J., Davies, M., Roberts, W. and Morrison, T. (1986) 'The Towers of Silence: Creative and Destructive Issues for Therapeutic Teams Dealing with Sexual Abuse', *Journal of Family Therapy*, 8, pp 1–25.

Dejong, A., Hervada, A. and Emmett, G. (1983) 'Epidemiologic Variations in Childhood Sexual Abuse', *Child Abuse and Neglect*, 7, pp. 155–62.

Eardley, T. (1985) 'Violence and Sexuality', in A. Metcalf and M. Humphries (eds) *The Sexuality of men*, London, Pluto Press.

Eichenbaum, L. and Orbach, S. (1982) *Outside In. . . Inside Out*, Harmondsworth, Penguin.

165

Farrell, C. (1978) *My Mother Said . . . The Way Young People Learned about Sex and Birth Control* London, Routledge & Kegan Paul.

Finkelhor, D. (1979) *Sexually Victimised Children*, New York, Free Press.

Finkelhor, D. (1984) *Child Sexual Abuse*, New York, Free Press.

Frosh, S. (1987a) *The Politics of Psychoanalysis*, London, Macmillan.

Frosh, S. (1987b) 'Issues for Men Working with Sexually Abused Children', *British Journal of Psychotherapy*, 3, pp. 332–9.

Furniss, T. (1983) 'Mutual Influence and Interlocking Professional–Family Process in the Treatment of Child Sexual Abuse and Incest', *Child Abuse and Neglect*, 7, pp. 207–23.

Furniss, T. (1984) 'Conflict-Avoiding and Conflict-Regulating Patterns in Incest and Child Sexual Abuse', *Acta Paedopsychiat*, 50, pp. 299–313.

Furniss, T., Bingley-Miller, L. and Bentovim, A. (1984) 'Therapeutic Approach to Sexual Abuse', *Archives of Disease in Childhood*, 59, pp. 865–870.

Giaretto, H. (1977) 'Humanistic Treatment of Father–Daughter Incest', *Child Abuse and Neglect*, 1, pp. 411–26.

Giaretto, H. (1981) 'A Comprehensive Child Sexual Abuse Treatment Programme', in P. Mrazek and C. Kempe (eds) *Sexually Abused Children and their Families*, Oxford, Pergamon Press.

Glaser, D. and Collins, C. (1987) 'The Response of Non-Sexually-Abused Children to Anatomically Correct Dolls', *paper presented to the Association of Child Psychology and Psychiatry*.

Glaser, D., Furniss, T. and Bingley, L. (1984) 'Focal Family Therapy: the Assessment Stage', *Journal of Family Therapy*, 6, pp. 265–74.

Goldman, R. and Goldman, J. (1982) *Children's Sexual Thinking*, London, Routledge & Kegan Paul.

Goodwin, J. (1982) *Sexual Abuse: Incest Victims and their Families*, Littleton, Mass., PSG Publishing Co.

Hall, R. (1985) *Ask Any Woman: A London Inquiry into Rape and Sexual Assault*, Bristol, Falling Wall Press.

Herman, J. (1981) *Father–Daughter Incest*, Cambridge, Harvard University Press.

Herman, J, and Hirschman, L. (1977) 'Father–Daughter Incest', *Signs*, 2, pp. 1–22.

Hobbs, C, and Wynne, J. (1986) 'Buggery in Childhood: A Common Syndrome of Child Abuse', *Lancet*, 2, pp. 792–6.

Hollway, W. (1984) 'Gender Difference and the Production of Subjectivity', in J. Henriques, W. Hollway, C. Urwin, C. Venn and V. Walkerdine, *Changing the Subject*, London, Methuen.

Howells, K. (1979) 'Some Meanings of Children for Paedophiles', in M. Cook and G. Wilson (eds) *Love and Attraction*, Oxford, Pergamon.

Jackson, S. (1982) *Childhood and Sexuality*, Oxford, Blackwell.

Jones, D. P. H. and Krugman, R. (1986) 'Can a Three-Year-Old Child Bear Witness to Her Sexual Assault and Attempted Murder?', *Child Abuse and Neglect*, 10, pp. 253–8.

Jones, D. P. H. and McQuiston, M. (1985) *Interviewing the Sexually*

Abused Child, Denver, The C. Henry Kempe National Center for the Prevention and Treatment of Child Abuse and Neglect.

Justice, B. and Justice R. (1979) *The Broken Taboo: Sex in the Family*, New York, Human Sciences Press.

Kempe, R. and Kempe, C. (1978) *Child Abuse*, London, Fontana.

Langevin, R. (ed.) (1985) *Erotic Preference, Gender Identity and Aggression in Men*, New Jersey, Lawrence Erlbaum.

Miller, A. (1984) *Thou Shalt Not Be Aware*, London, Pluto.

Mitchell, J. (1974) *Psychoanalysis and Feminism*, Harmondsworth, Penguin.

Mrazek, P., Lynch, M. and Bentovim, A. (1983) 'Sexual Abuse of Children in the United Kingdom', *Child Abuse and Neglect*, 7, pp. 147–53.

Nelson, S. (1987) *Incest: Fact and Myth*, Edinburgh, Stramullion.

Newson, J. and Newson, E. (1963) *Patterns of Infant Care in an Urban Community*, London, Allen & Unwin.

Penn, P. (1982) 'Circular Questioning' *Family Process*, 21, pp. 267–80.

Pierce, R. and Pierce, L. (1985) 'The Sexually Abused Child: A Comparison of Male and Female Victims', *Child Abuse and Neglect*, 9, pp. 191–9.

Renvoize, J. (1982) *Rape in Marriage*, New York, Macmillan.

Russell, D. (1983) 'The Incidence and Prevalence of Intrafamilial Sexual Abuse of Female Children', *Child Abuse and Neglect*, 7, pp. 133–46.

Rutter, M. (1983) 'Psychosexual Development' in M. Rutter (ed.) *Scientific Foundations of Developmental Psychiatry*, London, Heinemann.

Schechter, M. and Roberge, L. (1976) 'Child Sexual Abuse', in R. Helter and C. Kempe (eds) *Child Abuse and Neglect: The Family and the Community*, Cambridge, Mass., Ballinger.

Schofield, M. (1965) *The Sexual Behaviour of Young People*, London, Longman.

SCOSAC (1984) 'Definition of Child Sexual Abuse', *Standing Committee on Sexually Abused Children*, London.

Sears, R., Maccoby, E. and Levin, H. (1957) *Patterns of Child Rearing*, New York, Harper & Row.

Seidler, V. (1985) 'Fear and Intimacy', in A. Metcalf and M. Humphries (eds) *The Sexuality of Men*, London, Pluto Press.

Straus, M., Gelles, R. and Steinmetz, S. (1981) *Behind Closed Doors: Violence in the American Family*, New York, Anchor.

Summit, R. (1983) 'The Child Sexual Abuse Accommodation Syndrome', *Child Abuse and Neglect*, 7, pp. 177–93.

Tsai, M., Feldman-Summers, S. and Edgar, M. (1979) 'Childhood Molestation: Variables Related to Differential Impact on Psychosexual Functioning in Adult Women', *Journal of Abnormal Psychology*, 88, pp. 407–17.

Tsai, M. and Wagner, N. (1978) 'Therapy Groups for Women Sexually Molested as Children', *Archives of Sexual Behaviour*, 7, pp. 417–27.

Walmsley, R. and White, K. (1979) *Sexual Offences, Consent and Sentencing*, Home Office Research Study 54, London, HMSO.

Ward, E. (1984) *Father–Daughter Rape*, London, The Women's Press.
Weeks, J. (1985) *Sexuality and its Discontents*, London, Routledge & Kegan Paul.
Weinberg, S. (1955) *Incest Behavior*, New Jersey, Citadel Press (reprinted 1976).
West, D. (1985) *Sexual Victimisation*, New York, Gower.
Wild, N. J. (1986) 'Sexual Abuse of Children in Leeds', *British Medical Journal*, 292, pp. 1113–16.
Wyatt, G. (1985) 'The Sexual Abuse of Afro–American and White–American Women in Childhood', *Child Abuse and Neglect*, 9, pp. 507–19.

Index

169